Awesome
ANCIENT
GRAINS
& Seeds

DAN JASON and MICHELE GENEST

Awesome ANCIENT GRAINS *&Seeds*

A GARDEN-TO-KITCHEN GUIDE

Includes 50 Vegetarian Recipes

Douglas & McIntyre

Dedication

This book is dedicated to everyone helping to preserve our treasure of heritage seeds

Copyright © 2018 Dan Jason and Michele Genest

1 2 3 4 5 — 22 21 20 19 18

Douglas and McIntyre (2013) Ltd.
P.O. Box 219, Madeira Park, BC, V0N 2H0
www.douglas-mcintyre.com

Photos by Christina Symons unless otherwise noted
Top front cover photo by Karen Mouat. All other cover photos by Christina Symons

Edited by Carol Pope
Indexed by Nicola Goshulak
Cover and text design by Diane Robertson

Printed and bound in China

Douglas and McIntyre (2013) Ltd. acknowledges the support of the Canada Council for the Arts, which last year invested $153 million to bring the arts to Canadians throughout the country. We also gratefully acknowledge financial support from the Government of Canada and from the Province of British Columbia through the BC Arts Council and the Book Publishing Tax Credit.

Library and Archives Canada Cataloguing in Publication

Jason, Dan, author

     Awesome ancient grains & seeds : a garden-to-kitchen guide : includes 50 vegetarian recipes / by Dan Jason and Michele Genest.

Includes index.
Issued in print and electronic formats.
ISBN 978-1-77162-177-9 (softcover).--ISBN 978-1-77162-178-6 (HTML)

1. Grain. 2. Seeds. 3. Cooking (Cereals). 4. Cooking (Seeds). 5. Vegetarian cooking. 6. Cookbooks. I. Genest, Michele, author II. Title.

TX808.J37 2018   641.6'31   C2017-906338-3
                                      C2017-906339-1

ACKNOWLEDGEMENTS

Heartfelt acknowledgement of the love, support and inspiration that keep growing from my wife, Celeste, and my children, Zama, Toby, Peter, Leif and Naomi. Thank you to my best gardening buddies, Raven Hume, Rinda Lim, Rick Abramyk, Elly Silverman and Rupert Adams. Huge appreciation and thank you once again to Carol Pope for her skilful and wonderful editing work.

—*Dan Jason*

Thank you to Dan Jason and to all the farmers and gardeners who are bringing back and sharing the ancient knowledge, and to my fellow cooks and expeditionaries Lyn Fabio and Yvette Nolan. Special thanks to Hector MacKenzie, always up for the adventure!

—*Michele Genest*

Contents

Recipes

FOREWORD

Stepping back to the wisdom of the ages, Dan Jason—lifelong food activist and founder of Salt Spring Seeds, a heritage-seed mainstay for organic food growers—takes us on an inspiring journey to meet and greet some of the most astounding superfoods of all time. Easy to grow and deeply satisfying to eat, these ancient grains and seeds are the nutritional powerhouses that sustained civilizations for thousands of years.

Amaranths and quinoas, revered by the Aztecs and Incas, along with ancient wheats, barleys, buckwheats, flaxseeds, soybeans, ryes and oats, are very much today as they always were: remarkably rich in protein, carbohydrates, essential fatty acids, vitamins, minerals and antioxidants when eaten as the whole foods they are. Add to this a modern twist on a ten-thousand-year-old theme—Styrian pumpkin's abundant hulless seeds are higher in health benefits than any other variety of the venerable squash family and an amazing addition to both garden and kitchen.

The bestselling author of such classics as *Saving Seeds as if Our Lives Depended On It* and *Some Useful Wild Plants*, along with the highly acclaimed *The Power of Pulses: Saving the World with Peas, Beans, Chickpeas, Favas and Lentils*, Dan has spent more than three decades searching out, testing and sharing how best to eat the most reliable, enjoyable and eco-logically friendly foods we can grow for ourselves. The ancient grains and

Opposite, clockwise from top: Elly is harvesting six-row barley that has awns twice as long as the seed heads. The Golden flax plants on the left have almost finished flowering, while the sunflowers have more weeks to shine. It's summer-time and the growing is easy. *All photos by Karen Mouat*

seeds explored in this book provide deep nourishment, the opportunity for greater self-sufficiency, and a simple and gratifying way of living sustainably in our modern-day world. Readily grown in elegant swaths in any yard or as stately clumps in large containers, these crops are easier to cultivate than garden greens, roots or fruits.

Complemented by Dan's peppering of ideas for quick snacks and suppers, an inspiring collection of recipes has been developed by Michele Genest, award-winning author of the bestselling cookbooks *The Boreal Gourmet* and *The Boreal Feast*. In a process of discovery guided by Dan's approach in his definitive *Salt Spring Seeds Cookbook*, Michele has focused on imaginative vegetarian dishes for gatherings of family and friends, inspired by cuisines from around the world.

Everyone can benefit from incorporating more whole grains and seeds into their diet, and the tempting recipes in this book provide a wonderful incentive. For both those who grow them from scratch and those who prefer to source them from their local market, these grains and seeds are amazingly versatile in the kitchen. Using ingredients commonly available to most Canadians, each recipe pays tribute to a time-honoured grain or seed, for a repertoire that results in a perfect balance of quick-to-fix and more elaborate dishes for a special occasion. Throughout the sections—Breakfast; Appetizers; Soups; Hearty Salads and Main Dishes; Breads, Flatbreads and Crackers; and Cookies, Cakes, Bars and Desserts—you will find many fresh surprises along with unforgettable old favourites, all deliciously celebrating the generous and nourishing bounty of these amazing ancient superfoods to grow and eat!

—Carol Pope
Associate Editor

PREFACE

I've been growing, eating and getting to know the crops in this book for the past thirty years. Each in its own way has become very special to me. I believe that these ancient foods hold rich and abundant promise for making old wisdom new again, showing us sustainable ways of living on our planet.

All these heritage grains and seeds have been cultivated and revered for thousands of years. However, we now seem to be missing the boat by turning them into lesser versions of themselves. When we choose to spend vast amounts of energy and resources to process, transport and package them, instead of appreciating them as they are—for maximum benefit—we lose an amazing food opportunity. Grains and seeds are all whole foods that are powerhouses of nutrition. They epitomize simplicity and efficiency, beauty, abundance and community, as seeds that have been handed down for hundreds of generations.

I am very blessed to have lived with these crops for the past three decades. I feel privileged and honoured to share the basic, yet little-known wisdom that they impart. The chapters that follow recount how these precious heritage crops—all of which are easy to grow, and so easy to eat— have taught me how much they have to offer.

I believe that there is an enormous elephant in the room in these fragile times, an obvious truth that few are willing to address. If humans are going to continue inhabiting Earth, we will have to figure out how to feed ourselves differently than we are doing now. The grains and seeds in this book have a lot to reveal to us about that!

—Dan Jason

CHAPTER 1

Saving the World
WITH GRAINS AND SEEDS

In researching the histories of the grains and seeds described in this book, I've had one big surprise. All the agricultural books and articles I had read over the years led me to believe that these seed crops had been selected and developed over centuries, by patient farmers and scientists, to become the foods we have today. Although there is some truth to that, archaeological studies have now made it clear that diverse amaranths, quinoas, wheats,[1] barleys, buckwheat, flaxseed, soybeans, ryes and oats were already in existence during the so-called Dawn of Agriculture, when stone tools were developed during the Neolithic Age.[2] Where these seeds and grains came from is, to my mind, a profound mystery that only underscores their great gift to humanity.

ANCIENT INDEED

These ancient seeds were not some "primitive" version of modern cultivars. Six to ten thousand years ago, they grew essentially as they do today, and are not significantly different from the seeds we grow now.[3]

In many cases, however, we have been depleting the whole goodness of these heritage grains and seeds by creating nutritionally inferior varieties for commercial interests and purposes. Modern agriculture takes pride in

Opposite: These amaranth plants will be higher than Amy in a few more weeks.
Karen Mouat photo

AWESOME ANCIENT GRAINS AND SEEDS

breads that hardly deteriorate with age, and in crops that have been bioengineered to withstand showers of herbicides.

But from how many new major crops created by science and technology have we truly benefitted? There is only one that I know and grow—and that is triticale, a cross between wheat and rye that combines attributes of both.

The more I think about it, the more I am awed by the ancient foods celebrated in this book—foods that have nourished and sustained people in temperate climates for countless generations.

I have grown, harvested and eaten these ancient grains and seeds for thirty years. It takes going through many seasons with these remarkable plants to begin to sense how many hands their seeds have passed through before they got to mine. Tough survivors, they provide so many stories and adventures each growing season. I regard these ancient foods as keys to living wisely, well and harmoniously on this planet. Why not continue to work for their optimum preservation, enhancement and proliferation, to ensure our own?

SIMPLE, RICH NOURISHMENT

Most people in North America have forgotten or perhaps have never known that grains and seeds can be cooked as the whole foods they are. You don't need to mill, pearl or roll them; just cook them to get all their goodness.

The grains and seeds I know and grow are rich in protein, carbohydrates, oils, vitamins, minerals and antioxidants. And they provide high percentages of the recommended daily requirements, unlike most processed and packaged foods found on supermarket shelves. Each of these grains and seeds is unique, and all have been revered by cultures around the world.

Their basic preparation requires very little time, although recipes using them vary from simple to elaborate. Flax and pumpkin seeds can be enjoyed raw or added to a multitude of cooked dishes. Grains and soybeans need only to be heated to boiling in the appropriate volume of water and simmered until cooked. If you don't count the cooking time, the actual preparation is but a few minutes!

These cooked whole grains and seeds are rich and substantial, and may be enhanced with small amounts of your favourite

Opposite: The seeds of Faust barley are very easy to separate from their hulls when it comes time to thresh them. Dan Jason photo

Above left: Long awns on grains can give them a graceful nodding effect. *Above right:* Rows of grains have magical ways of reflecting sunlight. *Both photos by Karen Mouat*

salts and seasonings. You can take meals a little further with some of the simple suggestions I offer—or go for gusto with Michele Genest's many beautiful and delicious recipes included in this book!

A VERY SOFT FOOTPRINT

"Carbon footprint" and "greenhouse-gas emissions" are two phrases we often hear these days in relation to human activities and their damaging impact upon the possibility of a sustainable future for us all. When discussing climate change, our politicians earnestly talk about cars and coal, but seldom seem to mention our diet as a massive contributor to greenhouse-gas emissions.

The crops described in this book have a very soft footprint (minimal impact) when grown in home gardens or on small acreages without biocides and synthetic fertilizers.[4] While growing, the plants draw up minerals from the subsoil and, when finished, they add organic matter to the soil that helps to prevent its erosion.

Consider, on the other hand, the amount of energy it takes to keep industrial agriculture going: the huge machinery required to plant, maintain and harvest crops; the planes used in aerial spraying; and the trucks that deliver the harvest to storage and processing plants, and then to markets.

Even more harmful are genetically modified seeds and grains, which leave a deep carbon footprint and create greenhouse-gas

emissions. Forests and jungles are burned to make room for the planting of genetically modified organisms (GMOs), while protests by concerned citizens often are suppressed. Millions of acres are dedicated to crops grown for junk-food products and fast food fare. Worse still, the land becomes degraded almost beyond redemption by an endless application of poisons.

Why not grow our own crops or eat local produce, instead of ruining the planet? With wise food choices, each of us can help to fight climate change with every meal that sustains us. It's time that we appreciate not only the nourishment homegrown whole grains and seeds provide, but the energy *not* spent when we grow our own.

Above left: Soybeans are as easy to grow as pinto or kidney beans. *Karen Mouat photo. Above right:* Try sprouting your grain and seed crops to add healthy, fresh flavour to salads, sandwiches, and stir-fries. See Chapter II (page 89) for instructions

CHAPTER 2

Growing Your Own
GRAINS AND SEEDS

The beauty of the grains and seeds I talk about in this book can win you over in just a season. I've come to be totally smitten by their grace and elegance, their solidity and resilience, their brilliance of design and their astonishing power.

I recommend that you try growing each of these seeds and grains at least once, simply to experience them and to eat them from your own garden. Even one season's intimacy with these nourishing whole foods, so deeply rooted in human history, can change your relationship to them forever. Having become so well acquainted with them, you'll greet these precious seeds and grains with remembrance and gratitude whenever they are on your plate.

SOWING IS EASY

Even though these ancient crops are rarely offered by garden-seed companies other than Salt Spring Seeds,[5] they are easier to grow than beets or carrots, lettuces or spinach, tomatoes or peppers. As you'll see in the sections about growing provided in each chapter, they all can be sown directly into the earth at the appropriate time. These seeds and grains do well in a wide range of soils, need very little thinning, require little maintenance and have few pests. All that adds up to super-easy gardener's delight!

Opposite: Grains look just like grass as they get growing. Karen Mouat photo

ORNAMENTAL BLISS

From glorious amaranth and quinoa to ancient barleys and wheats, from buckwheat and soybeans to flax and grand Styrian pumpkin, the plants featured in this book are valuable both for the highly nourishing food they offer and for their beauty in the garden.

Grow drought-resistant amaranth and quinoa under eaves or along a fence line to enjoy plumes of vibrant colour. Scatter flax into an empty bed for a sea of blue, or treat the bees to buckwheat's froth of flowers. Give elegant striped Styrian pumpkin some room to sprawl, and soybeans a sunny spot in which to luxuriate. Try ancient grains in swaths or stately clumps in big pots. Or toss the seeds of barley, rye, triticale or wheat over bare earth in early spring or at summer's end, to safeguard the soil as the rains begin.

PROTECTING PRECIOUS SOIL

As well as looking good, these plants give generously to the ecosystem of the organic garden—attracting helpful bees, boosting nitrogen, tolerating drought, adding mulch or reducing soil erosion.

Grains make particularly excellent compost and mulch material. After the seed heads are harvested, the straw can be cut down and allowed to decompose into a nourishing additive to boost the

health of soil and to help it retain moisture. Or lay out the straw as attractive mulch around other food crops.

YOUR SEEDS ARE ALREADY SAVED

Not only are these ancient crops easier to grow than garden greens, roots and fruits, but saving seeds from them is as simple as can be.

To harvest seeds from annual vegetables, such as lettuce, spinach and tomatoes, you need to wait many weeks past their eating stage. Biennials, such as carrots, beets and kale, require overwintering before they flower and go to seed.

Happily, for all the crops in this book, your intended harvests are the seeds themselves. They ripen in only three to four months, and saving seeds for future sowings is just a matter of not eating all of them.

Stored in airtight containers in a cool and dry place, away from light, all the grains and seeds in this book should remain viable for at least five years.

Above left: Globes of flaxseeds become dry and brittle as they ripen. *Karen Mouat photo. Above right:* Tibetan barley is extremely hardy. *Dan Jason photo*

CHAPTER 3

Amaranth

As a seed crop that reproduces itself so magnificently and magnanimously, amaranth (*Amaranthus* spp.) has no peer. Amaranth's ability to thrive with or without moisture is unsurpassed by any other food plant I know. And, if you're trying to find the best crop to prevent starvation in the most places on Earth, under the most conditions, amaranth is it.

A TALENT FOR SURVIVAL

Early on, during my first trials of amaranth in 1986, I decided to see how it would do on a small, dried-out hillside. As it had rained only slightly that summer, there was no moisture in the soil. Responding to these drought conditions, the amaranth developed side roots that soaked up the morning dew. The 24 plants, each 6 feet (180 cm) tall—although they would have been 8 feet (250 cm) tall in richer soil—yielded 17 pounds (7.7 kg) of seed. Amaranth had me hooked—and still does!

ABUNDANCE OF AMARANTH

To this day, I harvest small patches of amaranth with a rubbing-and-shaking method, and take delight in the first rainfalls of seed drumming into the bottom of my bucket. My amazement at the yields led me to research how much seed could normally be expected from a single plant. (You'd never want to try counting them by hand!)

I eventually learned from Frank Morton of Wild Garden Seed in Oregon that the accepted figure for amaranth is thirty thousand seeds per

Opposite: Amaranth flowers vary considerably depending on the cultivar. *Karen Mouat photo*

Above: Red amaranth in flower. *Photo courtesy Esben_H/Thinkstock*

ounce.[6] Weighing the harvest of three of my larger plants, I now know that *half a million seeds can be harvested from a single amaranth plant!*

The question sometimes comes to me: "If you planted every seed harvested from one amaranth plant, and then planted every seed from each of the resulting plants the following year, how much would you get?" I admit I give up trying to wrap my mind around the number, but I know this to be true: you would get a vast amount of highest-quality food—and wouldn't *that* solve a lot of problems in the world!*

A PLAN FOR FAMINE PREVENTION

During my early years of promoting amaranth, it seemed to me that I was the only one doing so. Then, in 1991, I bought a

* Editor's note: Under ideal conditions with a 100 percent germination rate, one could harvest over 118 million metric tons of seed!

copy of *Save Three Lives: A Plan for Famine Prevention* by Robert Rodale,[7] author, publisher and crusader for organic gardening. This book highlighted amaranth as the most extraordinary crop for ease of growing, excellent nutrition and potential for solving the problem of famine in drought-prone countries. While this last book of Rodale's may not be well known, it has kept me focused on my own amaranth mission all these years.

I still believe that amaranth will one day reign supreme in North America—as well as in many other regions of the world, where it could solve the tragedy of hunger. In fact, because of its high nutritional value and ability to grow in the toughest of conditions, amaranth seed has now been put on the menu for NASA's space-shuttle missions.[8]

SYMBOL OF IMMORTALITY

Thought to be around eight thousand years old, amaranth has been a symbol of immortality since the time of ancient Greece. Derived from the Greek word *amarantos*, its name means "unwithering" and refers to the plant's spectacular flowers—which last until hard frost and continue to bloom even as the flower heads turn to seed.

Amaranth was also revered in Central and South America.[9] Native to Peru, amaranth has been found in Andean tombs more than four thousand years old. The Incas called it *kiwicha*, and considered it a great blessing of Mother Earth.[10] Amaranth was such a significant part of their culture that the Spaniards outlawed its use when they conquered the Incas in 1533.

Amaranth was also ritualized as a sacred plant by the Aztecs, who called their most important food *huautli*. As with the Incas, its use by the Aztecs was ruthlessly suppressed after the Spanish conquest. Now, almost five hundred years later, amaranth is having a major revival in Peru, Bolivia and Mexico.

These seeds probably also were gathered from wild plants by hunter-gatherers in early North America, but were mostly forgotten here too—until the 1970s, when cultivated plants were introduced.[11] Amaranth's nourishing seeds are also catching people's attention now in Asian, African and European countries, where previously only the leaves were eaten.

AWESOME ANCIENT GRAINS AND SEEDS

EAT THE LEAVES

Amaranth greens are valued in Mediterranean and African countries, as well as in China, India and Mexico. Perhaps "greens" is not an accurate descriptor, because the leaves of many amaranth cultivars are red, gold or purple. Like spinach or chard, they can be steamed, stir-fried, sautéed, tossed in pasta and added to soups.

Amaranth leaves taste sweeter and are much higher in calcium, phosphorus and vitamin C than spinach or chard.[12] Fresh young leaves can add nutrition and excitement to a salad but are best used from plants no older than a month or so. Older leaves become very chewy. For cooking, slighter older leaves are fine. You'll always find lots on each amaranth plant. In fact, after thirty to forty days, you can cut off the entire top of the plant and eat it. The plant will quickly grow secondary stalks. Once amaranth has flowered, the leaves get a bit tougher but are still very good when freshly cooked. One thing to note is that they aren't very good when reheated.

EXCEPTIONAL, GLUTEN-FREE NUTRITION

Amaranth's broad leaves indicate that it's not really a grain like wheat or barley. Technically, it's a pseudocereal, a non-grass plant that produces seed or fruit that can be consumed as grains. Nevertheless, the seed of amaranth is often referred to as a grain—despite the fact that the nutritional profile of amaranth seed is much richer than that of our common grains.

In my early days of growing amaranth, I was inspired upon reading that the seed comes closer to fully meeting the accepted protein requirements of the human body than cow's milk does, and that it has twice the amount of calcium as milk[13] and an essential amino acid balance[14] that is near ideal.[15] It is high in alpha-linolenic acid (a plant-based omega-3 fatty acid often referred to as ALA), high in fibre, and a rich source of phytosterols, which are given credit for lowering cholesterol in the body.[16]

Amaranth seed also is notably high in the amino acid known as lysine, which is lacking in most cereals (such as wheat, sorghum, corn and barley).[17] It is an excellent source of fibre and of the B vitamins thiamine, riboflavin, niacin, B_6, folate and pantothenic

Opposite: These amaranth leaves are at a good stage for steamed greens. *Karen Mouat photo*

acid. Amaranth is impressively high in manganese, magnesium, iron, selenium, phosphorus, calcium and zinc, and has appreciable amounts of vitamins C and E.[18] It does not contain gluten, and so can be ground into a gluten-free flour.[19]

Amaranth seed also has advantages in terms of its cooking and preparation. It cooks up in just 10 to 12 minutes, simmered in an equal volume of water. Its mild, pleasant taste allows for great versatility. It can be sweetened as a good-start breakfast cereal, or served as a satisfying side dish with or without your favourite oil, herbs or sauce. Added to almost any dish, it will make a meal more nutritious.

HARVESTING BY HAND

Considering its amazing assets, why hasn't amaranth caught on yet as a superfood?

I think the main reason that amaranth is still so expensive and relatively unknown in North America is that it is not easily harvested by large-scale threshing equipment. It needs dry weather and frosty nights so that the seeds can be combined cleanly. Traditional hand-harvesting usually out-yields the harvests obtained by big machinery.

It took me quite a few years to learn to follow the example set by small birds and to harvest amaranth before it dries down on the plant. When the seeds are ripe, they fall easily from the flower heads with just a little jiggling. I rub the seed heads briskly between my hands over a bucket, tapping them against the sides and letting them plunk in. This method differs from seed saving for every other crop I grow; for them, it is important to get the seeds when they are really dry.

Since amaranth takes almost no time to cultivate and to maintain, surely we can figure out ways of recruiting people to harvest it on a commercial scale. And, most certainly, this is an ideal food plant for home gardeners!

AN UNFORGETTABLE GARDEN PLANT

Growing amaranth is a thrilling experience. Even as you're watching, it's hard to believe that such a little seed could grow such a big plant so quickly. In just a few months, amaranth plants can tower over your head!

Opposite, clockwise from top: Starting amaranth in potting soil gives plants a head start for when the garden soil warms up. Amaranth leaves get lighter as the seeds ripen. After rubbing amaranth through a coarse screen, the seeds can be separated from the chaff with a finer screen. All photos by Dan Jason

They are very hardy and adaptable, as well. So hardy, in fact, that some weedy relatives of cultivated amaranth can't be killed by herbicide.[20] One of these common weeds, *Amaranthus palmeri*, also provides edible seeds and greens (if you find it in a spray-free area).[21]

Amaranth self-sows quite readily and, in climates of zone 8 or warmer, could almost be considered a perennial plant when left alone. Its timing seems to be just right for optimal growth. Leave it wherever you would like it to stay; otherwise, it is easy to pull out. Or, if the spot is not large enough for a full-sized plant, let it grow for a while and then yank it to harvest the greens.

Amaranth's copious leaf and seed production can provide a lot of aesthetic and culinary delight with just a few plants. In terms of placement in a garden, considerations are the same as for tall sunflowers; you'd normally think of growing them at the back of beds or against a sunny fence. But you can also consider using amaranth to shade other heat-sensitive plants, such as spinach and lettuce, from direct sun. Or tuck in shallow-rooted flowers like nasturtiums or calendula around their base.

Varieties. Seed catalogues usually list varieties of seed amaranth according to the colour of the flowers. I've seen Bronze, Burgundy, Dark Red, Garnet Red, Giant Purple, Golden, Lotus Purple, Orange Giant and Red Beauty. These generally are tall, upright plants with huge flower heads. Leaves are green in some varieties, purple in others.

Amaranth seeds look like miniature sesame seeds, and can be white or black. Up until a few years ago, I shunned the black-seeded cultivars because they were gritty when cooked, compared to the white-seeded varieties. Then I discovered a black amaranth that had a much better texture. Not only that, but the seeds smell like chocolate as they cook, have a sweet flavour and appealing aftertaste, and are delicious in both savoury and dessert dishes. I call this variety Shiny Black Amaranth because the dark seeds have a dazzling golden shine.

Other amaranths that I grow and also feature in the Salt Spring Seeds catalogue are Bronze, Purple and Amaranth Mix.

Some amaranths used only for greens are Tampala, Calaloo, Red Perilla and Chinese Spinach.

Soil and Sun. The optimum soil for growing amaranth is well drained and loamy. Nitrogen and phosphorus help to stimulate its growth. However, amaranth will do well in all but poorly aerated clay soils. Place it where it will receive more than six hours a day of full sun.

Planting Time. The best germination occurs when soil temperatures range from 65 to 75F (18 to 24C). For southern Canada and the northern US, this usually means a late-May or early-June planting.

I like to direct-sow amaranth in the ground, but if you want to get a head start, tuck a few seeds in a flat of organic potting mix to start inside and scoop out the seedlings for planting in the garden once they have produced two to three leaves. Before transplanting, loosen the soil where they are to go as much as you can, to accommodate their vigorous roots. If you start them in small pots, transplant the baby amaranths before the roots start showing through the drain holes of their containers.

Sowing. The small seeds of amaranth will germinate more successfully with a finely prepared surface. Seeds should be no more than ¼ inch (0.6 cm) deep. When I'm sowing a long row, I use my row seeder and barely cover the seeds. It's fairly impossible to sow the seeds one by one, so a very light scattering is best. A shallow groove made with a rake or hoe helps in creating straight lines.

Above left: Amaranth plants can get quite massive without irrigation. *Above right:* These Red amaranths are adding to a glorious sunset. *Both photos by Dan Jason*

The seeds could also be surface-sown in patches and tamped down lightly. Since the seed is tiny, you can avoid considerable thinning by mixing it with sand.

If planting more than a single line of amaranth, allow 18 to 24 inches (46 to 61 cm) between rows, to create a walking space between plants. This distance is also wide enough to accommodate a rototiller (for weed control) between the rows without damaging the plants. Plants should eventually be thinned so that they are 6 to 18 inches (15 to 46 cm) apart. Thinnings make great salad additions.

Maintenance. While amaranth is a low-maintenance plant, weeds should be discouraged by means of cultivation or mulching, particularly at the beginning of its growth. Amaranth resembles redroot pigweed, especially in the early stages. Sowing in rows makes it easier to spot this common weed, as does choosing cultivars with purple leaves.

Until mid-June, the soil's moisture is usually sufficient to germinate the seed. And once amaranth gets going, it rarely needs water. It is slow-growing at first, but extremely drought-tolerant. As the plants reach about 12 inches (30 cm) in height, they start to develop very rapidly and the canopy closes in, blocking out weeds and helping to retain moisture in the soil.

You may find minor munching by insect larvae in amaranth flower heads, but this won't have any serious impact upon the harvest. Use a hose to blast off insects, if you wish, or hand-pick them off. Or just leave them where they are; they won't bother sturdy amaranth!

Harvesting. Amaranth keeps on flowering until hit by the first hard frost. Seeds will often ripen many weeks before that, usually after about three months. The best way to determine if the seed is harvestable is to gently but briskly rub and shake the flower heads between your hands, to test whether seeds fall readily. You might see small birds at the flowers before you do this! Gather ripe seeds, in dry weather, by bending the plants over a bucket and using that rubbing-and-shaking motion.

I have seen online videos of hand-harvesting methods in Mexico and Kenya, where the long rows of amaranth are cut down, as I do it, while the huge heads are still in their glory. (The best time to harvest amaranth commercially with combines is in dry weather, three to seven days after first frost—a condition not easily met in many places.)

Threshing. Once you've gathered a harvest, it's a matter of running it through a fine mesh that screens the seeds from chaff. Or chaff can be removed by wind winnowing or with fans.

My own preferred threshing method is to rub the flower heads through a coarse screen and then a finer screen (just large enough to let the seeds through), into a wheelbarrow. Then I blow away the finer chaff using an air compressor. A blow dryer also works well.

It is far easier to thresh amaranth while the flowers are fresh and the seeds fall readily. Cutting and hanging plants to dry them indoors does not work very well; the plants become extremely bristly, making it difficult to separate seed from chaff.

After harvesting and threshing, it is important to dry your crop further, to ensure that it won't mould while in storage. It can be left on trays in a greenhouse or a bright warm room, or can be placed near an indoor heat source. Stir it occasionally, until it is as dry as possible. This will take longer than for other seed crops, which are harvested when they are already very dry. Four to six days of drying will probably be necessary for your amaranth seed.

Yields. You should be able to harvest a pound (0.45 kg) of seed from each amaranth plant.

Saving Seed. Amaranth can be cross-pollinated by its wild relative, so it is important to weed out redroot pigweed or common amaranth (*Amaranthus retroflexus*) if you want to maintain pure seed.

Amaranth cultivars will also cross with each other, so grow only one kind or separate cultivars by as much distance as you can if you want to protect your seed from being affected. Certain varieties, such as purple-leaved amaranth, are easier to select for than others. Still, I don't worry too much about my different amaranth cultivars crossing, as this doesn't seem to affect their quality or yield.

HOW TO ENJOY AMARANTH SEED

Amaranth seed is easy to digest and has a simple, distinctive taste that gives it great versatility for cooking purposes. It can be substituted for other grains in many recipes, though it is much more filling. Try it in many ways!

Hot Cereal. Unlike beans or true grains, amaranth has no hulls to remove, so it can be cooked without additional preparation. For cooked amaranth cereal, experiment to find the porridge-like texture you most enjoy. My preference is 12 minutes of simmering in an equal volume of water, but most sources mention a ratio of 2:1 water to seeds and 20 minutes of cooking time.

Side Dish. Cooked amaranth stands well as a side dish, to boost lunch and dinner meals. Here, you might prefer a less mushy texture than for morning cereal.

With Vegetables. Add cooked amaranth to a dish of cooked greens or to briefly sautéed celery, scallions or carrots.

Cook with Carrots. Simmer 1 cup (250 mL) carrots with 1 cup water and 1 cup amaranth for 12 minutes, for a ready-to-eat combination that may also be added to a soup, stew or stir-fry.

Use as Flour. Amaranth seed can be ground into a gluten-free flour that combines well with traditional flours, using a ratio of 1:4 amaranth to other grains.

Pop It! Amaranth seed can also be popped like popcorn, which results in a very different but no less delectable way of eating it. Popped amaranth is used in Mexico to make a sweet treat called *alegria* (which translates as "joy" or "happiness").

Just 1 tablespoon (15 mL) of amaranth seed will give you ⅓ cup (80 mL) after popping. Don't add oil or rinse the amaranth before popping it. A medium-sized stainless-steel pot works well. Heat the pot to medium-high or just below high heat. A drop of water that quickly evaporates when flicked into the pot will tell you when to add the amaranth. To prevent burning, it's best to add seeds 1 tablespoon (15 mL) at a time and to spread them uniformly over the bottom. Using oven mitts, quickly put the lid on and slide the pot back and forth as you would for popcorn. Amaranth pops very quickly, and most seeds will have popped within 10 seconds. Empty them into a bowl to cool. Repeat the process by putting the pot back on the burner to reheat.

Cooled popped amaranth can be stored for up to a month by putting it in a jar or sealed plastic bag in the refrigerator. Try eating a spoonful of your freshly popped amaranth. It's addictively good!

Because of its nutty taste and crunchy texture, popped amaranth can be added to many dishes for a satisfying and enriching protein hit. Enjoy it in these ways:

1. While both popped and cooked amaranth make a delightful breakfast cereal, popped amaranth doesn't get soggy. Add fruit, cinnamon and the milk of your choice.
2. Popped amaranth can be tossed into stews or onto salads.
3. Sprinkle it onto mashed potatoes.
4. Popped amaranth adds flavour and texture to cooked grains.
5. It sticks well to nut butters or cream cheese spread on sliced cucumbers or celery pieces.

CHAPTER 4

Barley

I started becoming interested in barley (*Hordeum vulgare*) in my early years as a seedsman, in the mid-1980s. While I knew it was a very significant crop in many countries and for numerous cultures, I was most impressed by its importance in Tibet. The Tibetan people, despite living in such a harsh climate, looked remarkably resilient and healthy—and it seemed to me that barley had a lot to do with their vitality.

SHORT-SEASON SUPERSTAR

One of the few grains that matures in less than three months, barley is a valuable food crop where the growing season is short. Another attribute that really caught my attention was that it is quite tolerant of freezing temperatures. One of the first cultivated grains, barley is so highly adaptable that it can be grown in climates ranging from subarctic to subtropical.

When I started testing varieties to see how they would respond to a September or October planting in the Pacific Northwest, I found that every cultivar could be fall-planted and relied on to make it through the winter, with a harvest in late June or early July. This enabled me to plant something else in that same space later, thus enjoying the benefit of two crops in one season.

HULLESS VS. HULLED

The barleys that most intrigued me were the so-called hulless types. While hulls cover all barley seeds, those on some hulless cultivars are loose

Opposite: Faust barley is both hulless and awnless. *Dan Jason photo*

Above left: Ethiopia preserves over six thousand barley cultivars in its Addis Ababa seed bank. *Dan Jason photo. Above right:* Karma Tibetan barley has purple heads and brownish-purple seeds. *Karen Mouat photo*

enough to rub off. I was hard-pressed to find these barleys in the mid-'80s; no seed companies seemed to have them.

A search eventually led to eight hulless varieties from the annual list of the Seed Savers Exchange in Decorah, Iowa.[22] I then figured out an easy method of separating the hulls at harvest: by rubbing them into a wooden box or rubber tub with my feet, instead of by hand! The hulless barleys were a big success, and I featured them in my Salt Spring Seeds catalogue because I thought they had great potential for the home gardener looking to become a more self-reliant food grower.

APPRECIATING BARLEY'S DIVERSITY

My eyes were really opened to the richness and diversity of barley one November day in 1993 in Ethiopia, when I was funded by USC Canada[23] to take their fifth annual Seeds of Survival course, along with "seed" people from all over Africa.

As one of the barleys I had acquired had originally come from Ethiopia, I found myself in the seed bank in Addis Ababa, very proudly and naively telling the Ethiopians there that I was growing Ethiopian barley. Well, they all burst into hysterical laughter for about ten minutes. Finally, my mentor, Melaku Worede, was able to tell me that they had more than six thousand cultivars of "Ethiopian" barley in the cold seed-storage room next door! They had barleys for different times of the day, barleys for brewing, barleys for thatching, barleys for animal food and barleys for special occasions such as funerals and weddings. Barley historically was a sacred crop for Ethiopia, and clearly still is.

Hearing what this barley diversity meant to another culture was a powerful experience for me. And so I added more barleys to my catalogue, including cultivars that needed to be processed by machinery, to free the seeds from the hulls.

BARLEY BREWING

In recent years, I've added quite a few malting barleys to my Salt Spring Seeds catalogue, thanks to my long-time friend, cohort and brewmaster, Rupert Adams. In barley brewing, the hulls are an important component because they aid the filtration of the brewer's extract during the lautering process. Hulless barley can sometimes gum up the filters, slowing down and adding to the cost of filtration.

Barley can be either two-row or six-row, depending upon the arrangement of the seed in the head when viewed down its axis. The two-row varieties lie flat, while six-row types are on three planes instead of two and present a fatter, more bulging head. Because two-row barley has less protein and a more fermentable sugar content, it's the best choice for brewmasters.

BARLEY'S PROVEN BENEFITS

As a versatile food, barley is appreciated across the globe for its nutritional benefits. A rich source of protein, fibre, thiamine, niacin, vitamin B_6, copper, selenium, manganese and phosphorus,[24] it is clearly a health booster.[25]

According to Health Canada and the Food and Drug Administration (FDA) in the US, consuming at least three grams (0.1 oz) of barley per day can lower levels of blood cholesterol[26] and can improve blood-sugar regulation. If eaten regularly, barley also greatly benefits cardiovascular health.[27] However, since barley contains gluten, it is unsuitable for people with gluten-related intolerances.

POT TO PEARL TO PORRIDGE

Hulled barley is eaten after removing the inedible outer hull. Once dehulled, it is often called "pot barley." Pot barley still has most of its bran and germ intact, making it a nourishing health food.

Pearl barley is dehulled, extra-polished and steam-processed to remove the bran, and may then be processed into a variety of products, including flour and oatmeal-like flakes.

Barley meal, a wholemeal barley flour, is cooked into porridge and gruel in Scottish households. The six-row variety Bere, cultivated in the Scottish Highlands, is used in bread, biscuits and bannock, as well as for brewing.

FROM THE ANCIENT MIDDLE EAST AND GREECE—UNTIL TODAY

With a history of cultivation in the Middle East that traces back to ancient times, barley was used in Assyrian, Israelite, Persian and Kurdish food preparation. Barley water, prescribed as a soothing remedy for those who were ill or overheated, dates back at least two thousand years, as a sacred part of Greek harvest celebrations.

Barley-meal gruel is known as *sawiq* in the Arab world. In Saudi Arabia, batches of barley soup are eaten during Ramadan. *Cholent,* or *hamin,* is a Jewish barley stew traditionally served on the Sabbath. And in Eastern and Central Europe, barley has long been added to soups.

Barley is also a highly respected food plant in Africa. The grains or flour are the main ingredient of a traditional cooling drink, called barley water or barley tea, found throughout Southeast Asia and China.

GROWS LIKE GRASS

As a garden crop, nothing is easier to cultivate or more rewarding than barley. It grows just like your lawn, but this beautiful and statuesque grass is left to mature rather than being mowed down.

Topped by awns, hair-like protuberances that arise from the seeds, barleys have a very pleasing appearance, especially when

they gracefully sway and dance in the wind. Awns vary in length and colour, ranging from golden-tinged varieties through bronze and reddish ones. There is even one cultivar, Faust, without awns. Awns are a great deterrent to foraging animals, making for an extremely unpleasant experience if stuck in the throat.

Varieties. If you're a gardener wanting to grow your own food, it is important to know the difference between hulled and hulless varieties, and to choose hulless ones.

Faust barley is one of my favourites, because it is both hulless and awnless. It is strikingly different from other barleys, is easy to thresh and has a mild earthy taste.

I also am partial to six-row hulless Purple barley because it has consistently been my most reliable producer and the kernels are so pretty.

My two-row Ethiopian hulless barley is also a high yielder, and reminds me of my time at the Ethiopian seed bank.

Above: Streaker barley is named for its "naked" hulless seeds. Karen Mouat photo

Soil and Sun. Barley grows well in ordinary garden soil, and its root growth makes it an excellent conditioner for both clay and sandy soil. It grows best with at least five or six hours of sun a day.

Planting Time. One of barley's best qualities is its hardiness. In much of North America, at a time when you normally wouldn't think of growing anything, it can be sown in the fall and over-wintered. And barley can serve as both a food crop and a cover crop that protects and enhances the soil.

On the west coast of British Columbia, I sometimes sow my barleys from late September through early November. They survive through very soggy times and nights that go down to 5F (-15C). Reports from seed customers across North America indicate that barley can withstand weather a lot colder than I get on my farm on Salt Spring Island.

If barley is not fall-planted, I recommend sowing it as soon as the ground can be worked in the spring. Grains benefit from an extended cooler season for growing and don't produce as well in late-spring plantings right before summer.

Sowing. It's a good idea for first-time grain growers to seed in rows, in prepared soil. This makes it easier to keep track of what you've planted when other grasses start appearing. You can make a slightly depressed line with a hoe, rake or stick to sow seeds by hand a few finger widths apart. I usually rely on my row seeder,

walking it through the row and setting the depth to a seed's length below the surface. You needn't worry about thinning.

After multiplying your crop for a season and learning what to expect, you might opt for planting in wide rows or blocks the next time. If planting in blocks or swaths in the garden, you could still plant in rows 3 to 4 inches (7.5 to 10 cm) apart, or you could scatter the seed and gently rake it under. As grains grow, they send out "tillers" or side shoots. Thus, single plants can quickly occupy open areas, making it harder for weeds to appear.

Maintenance. Weeding isn't as crucial for barley as it is for many other garden crops. While you will probably want to pull out other grasses to avoid confusion when harvesting, and to eliminate other bothersome weeds such as thistle and bindweed, barley is quite adept at colonizing areas once it gets going.

For spring-planted barley, water is also less a consideration than for other crops because there is usually abundant soil moisture when you plant. For fall-seeded crops—if it's a dry fall—you may need to irrigate your new plantings until rain returns.

Harvesting. Barley is ready for harvesting by the time it gets hot and dry in late June and July. With an early April sowing, my barleys are usually ready by late June or early July.

Harvest when the seed heads are completely dried. Your fingernail won't be able to dent a ripe grain kernel. You can snap the

Above left: Seeds should be dried until a fingernail can't make an indentation in them. *Karen Mouat photo. Above right:* This barley was named for the Ethiopian Queen of Sheba. *Dan Jason photo*

heads off with thumb and forefinger, or snip them with scissors into a bucket alongside.

Threshing. All manner of small-scale threshing equipment has been invented in countries where limited grain-growing is common. But until an inexpensive, efficient thresher appears on North American markets, I'm content to use my feet.

I've made a wooden box about 2 by 3 feet by 1 foot high (61 by 91 by 30 cm), with some thin slats screwed onto the inside bottom for extra abrasion. I step into my threshing box with the harvested grain and remove the hulls by the simple process of rubbing the grains against the bottom of the box with my shoes. This same shuffle performed in a Rubbermaid tub or on a tarp on flat ground would serve as well.

I then blow the chaff away with the nozzle attachment on my air compressor. A hair dryer, fan or even the wind will also work, or you can use appropriate screens. Any leftover chaff will rise to the water surface prior to cooking the grain, and can easily be skimmed off.

Yields. A 50-foot (15-m) row can easily yield 10 pounds (4.5 kg) of grain, while wide-row plantings can produce much more. Barley multiplies itself very rapidly. A small packet can end up being enough to sow an acre after two years' time!

Saving Seed. Barley cultivars don't cross, so saving seed for planting is simply a matter of not eating all the delicious harvest.

HOW TO ENJOY BARLEY

Barley is remarkably adaptable. Whether simmered, sprouted or raw, whether served as something to sip or as a nourishing supper, it is healthful and satisfying.

As a Beverage. Here is a recipe for barley water, which is used as a tonic for general illness and overheating, as an old-fashioned remedy for diarrhea and ulcers, and for stimulating breast milk. In a medium-sized saucepan, simmer 3 cups (710 mL) water and 2 tablespoons (30 mL) barley until reduced to 1½ cups (350 mL). Strain through a sieve, stir in 2 tablespoons (30 mL) lemon juice (and 1 to 2 tablespoons/15 to 30 mL honey, if desired) and simmer for 15 minutes.

Raw. You can eat whole barley uncooked if you soak the kernels overnight and then rinse them twice a day for two days. This gives you a raw food with a soft yet crunchy texture and a rich, sweet taste. These sprouted berries of grain are bursting with energy. They can be used in many delectable ways, from salads to wraps to soups to stir-fries.

Simmered. Whole barley takes about an hour's simmering to be cooked. Prior soaking speeds the process somewhat. Even with longer cooking, the texture will seem quite chewy to people accustomed to soft foods such as rice, pearled barley or rolled oats. Cooked whole grains generally are not eaten very quickly. I find their chewiness a definite attribute; it releases more flavour and expands meals to less hurried affairs.

Seasoned. Barley's earthy, musky flavour is enhanced by parsley, chives, bay leaves and basil. It combines well with bold seasonings such as fennel, garlic, anise, caraway, cloves, rosemary and thyme.

To Condense Soups and To Set Moulded Salads. Barley's thickening properties enrich soups and stews, and make it useful for moulded salads.

On the Side. Because of barley's assertive taste, it is best served as an accompaniment to meat, fish or dairy foods, instead of being mixed in with them.

Added In. Whole cooked barley also tastes wonderful when combined with pasta, lentils, mushrooms, peas, cabbage and carrots.

As Quick Dinners. Here are four simple meals for four, to which you can add some of your favourite herbs and seasonings:

1. **Barley/Veggie Combo:** Chop 2 carrots, an onion and a small parsnip or turnip. Dice a medium potato. Place these in a pot or casserole with 1 cup (250 mL) shredded cabbage and ½ cup (120 mL) whole barley. Add 2½ cups (600 mL) broth, stock or water, bring to a boil, cover and simmer for 1 hour. Salt and season to taste.

2. **Barley Pilaf:** Simmer 1 cup (250 mL) whole barley and 2⅔ cups (630 mL) vegetable stock in a covered pot for 1 hour. In a pan, sauté a sliced onion and finely chopped celery stalk in 2 tablespoons (30 mL) oil for about 5 minutes. Add 2 cups (475 mL) sliced mushrooms and sauté until mushrooms start to soften. Add the sauté to the cooked barley and simmer 5 to 10 more minutes, until liquid is absorbed. Add salt and favourite seasonings. Top with toasted Styrian pumpkin seeds for added zest.

3. **Barley with Pasta and Cabbage:** In a large skillet, sauté 1 cup (250 mL) chopped onion in 2 tablespoons (30 mL) oil until golden. Add 4 cups (1 L) finely chopped cabbage, and continue cooking until it wilts. Add 1 cup (250 mL) cooked barley and ½ cup (120 mL) cooked small pasta. Heat through. Season with salt, pepper and seasonings of choice.

4. **Barley and Beans:** Sauté a chopped onion in 2 tablespoons (30 mL) oil in a large saucepan until softened. Stir in 1⅓ cups (330 mL) of water, 1 cup (250 mL) salsa or taco sauce, ½ teaspoon (2.5 mL) ground cumin and ½ teaspoon (2.5 mL) crumbled oregano. Bring to a boil. Stir in ½ cup (120 mL) dry barley, and return to a boil. Cover and simmer for 1 hour. Stir in 1 cup (250 mL) cooked pinto or kidney beans. Simmer a few minutes longer until beans are heated through.

Opposite, from left to right, top row: Two-row Purple barley, Faust barley, Arabian Blue barley, Alba Winter barley. *Second row:* Belford barley, Bere barley, Excelsior barley, Gujar Khan barley. *Third row:* Full Pint Malting barley, Six-row Purple barley, Harrington Malting barley, Ethiopian barley. *Bottom row:* Himalayan barley, Robust barley, Sangatsuga barley, Karma Tibetan barley.

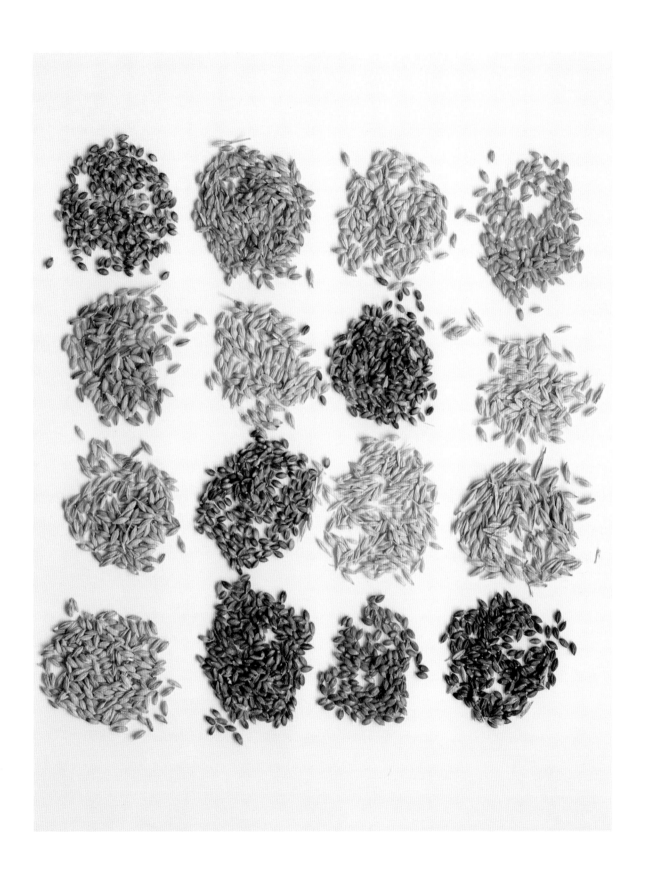

CHAPTER 5

Buckwheat

Buckwheat (*Fagopyrum tartarica*) is a multi-purpose plant I've cultivated since my early farming days. I've used it often as a cover crop, and relish eating it by sprouting its groats (the seeds when the outer shells are removed).

Sometimes I also pick off a few of the rutin-rich leaves to eat raw in salads or—tastier still—steamed as part of a meal. In fact, buckwheat seed collected from a home garden can be used to grow trays of nourishing buckwheat microgreens, called buckwheat "lettuce," indoors in a bright spot or under grow lights. (See page 95.)

I've never cooked up my own buckwheat seed, though, as this crop is not easy to thresh like the hulless wheats and barleys that I grow. Buckwheat's fruit is an achene, similar to a sunflower's, with a single seed inside a hard, dark outer hull. The hull is difficult for the home gardener to remove, but it is easy to remove commercially. The seed can then be freed from the thin ovary wall.

For hot cereal and nourishing suppers, I'm happy to use store-bought organic buckwheat groats grown by local farmers and hulled by commercial equipment. I also purchase organic buckwheat flour, for the best pancakes ever. (More about that later!)

BUCKWHEAT BLOOMS = BEES

In addition to buckwheat's edible greens and plantable seeds, there is another reason to plant this easy-grow crop in the garden: it provides tremendous support to bees.

Opposite: A field of buckwheat in flower. *Photo courtesy Zoonar RF/Thinkstock*

Above left: Buckwheat nearing the end of the flowering stage. *Photo courtesy Alter_photo/ Thinkstock. Above right:* Bees and other pollinators love buckwheat flowers, so stagger your plantings to provide continuous blooms for them. *Photo courtesy todaydesign/Thinkstock.*

Stagger plantings of buckwheat every three weeks, and you will be gifting your garden with wonderful buckwheat flowers that reliably attract many types of bees and other gentle pollinators. Buckwheat grows quickly and flowers prolifically for three weeks at a time. Plant it at these intervals and there will be continual flowering until first frost—along with the buzz of contentment from these essential insects that work hard to boost the productivity of our gardens.

RHUBARB'S RELATIVE

Despite its name, buckwheat is not a wheat or even a grain; in fact, this plant is related to sorrel and rhubarb. Like amaranth and quinoa, buckwheat is often referred to as a pseudocereal—a nongrass plant that produces seed or fruit—and is rich in proteins, carbohydrates, vitamins and minerals.

REVERED AND RITUALIZED

Like the other grains and seeds described in this book, buckwheat has been cultivated for thousands of years and is revered in several countries. Grown in inland Southeast Asia eight thousand years ago, it spread to Central Asia, Tibet, the Middle East, Europe and eventually to North America. In India, a special yearly Hindu festival, Navratri, features buckwheat in many of its traditional dishes. Not only is buckwheat delicious, but its easy digestibility and high nutritional value are both conducive to maintaining good health among those fasting during this time of celebration.

Russia and China are the world's largest producers of buckwheat. As wheat cannot be grown in high-mountain regions, buckwheat noodles have helped to sustain people from Tibet and northern China for centuries. These noodles also play a major role in the cuisines of Korea, northern Italy, and Japan (where they are often called "soba"). The difficulty of making soba noodles from flour containing no gluten has resulted in a traditional art that uses reverent, ritualistic movements to shape the noodles exquisitely by hand.

Also of note is kasha, a porridge made from roasted, hulled groats and brought to North America by Ukrainian, Polish and Russian immigrants. The cooked seeds are mixed with pasta or used as a filling for cabbage rolls, knishes and blintzes.

DUE FOR REVIVAL

Buckwheat used to be much more popular in North America than it is today. Then, in the middle of the twentieth century, along came industrial agriculture, with its high-nitrogen fertilizers. Buckwheat doesn't thrive with high-nitrogen inputs and so it was quickly replaced by crops that grow more productively with chemical fertilizers, such as wheat and barley.

I believe that buckwheat is due for a North American revival, as a highly nutritious and healthy food that does well even in poor soils. And it's an excellent choice for organic gardens.

NO GLUTEN; LOTS OF RUTIN

Besides being a rich source of protein, fibre and carbohydrates, buckwheat seed is high in manganese, copper, magnesium and phosphorus.[28] The protein in buckwheat contains all nine essential amino acids,[29] including lysine.[30] It is also a good source of iron,[31] thiamine, and vitamins C and E.

Buckwheat seed contains two flavonoids with significant health-promoting actions: rutin and quercetin.[32] In fact, buckwheat is the best natural source of rutin, which is said to keep blood vessels and capillaries healthy and flexible.[33] Because buckwheat contains no gluten, its flour may be eaten by people with gluten allergies or celiac disease.[34]

Studies on buckwheat have associated it with a lower risk of heart disease,[35] gallstones,[36] diabetes and breast cancer.[37]

A FAIR-WEATHER GARDEN FRIEND

Buckwheat is a fast-growing, sun-loving beauty that makes an excellent cover crop for any bare spot. Wherever you plant it, it will bring bees and beneficial insects.

Varieties. I favour Tartarian buckwheat because it's considered among the most edible and is also a superb fibre and protein food. It provides abundant seeds for growing greens and ample flowers for feeding bees.

Soil and Sun. While buckwheat is very easy to grow, unlike grains it is extremely susceptible to frost. It does best in warm weather, full sun and well-drained soil. It can also handle some drought. The soil need only be moderately fertile; in fact, buckwheat does better in acidic soil than other grain crops.

Planting Time. Plant in succession, every three weeks or so, once all danger of frost is over.

Sowing. Buckwheat can be sowed in block-planting areas by simply scattering the seed and gently raking it under. Alternatively, the triangular seed can be sprinkled a few inches apart in a shallow trough and covered lightly. If planted in rows, make them about 12 inches (30 cm) apart.

Maintenance. Buckwheat branches freely, and grows 30 to 50 inches (76 to 127 cm) tall. Because it establishes itself quickly, it is great at suppressing weeds. It reaches maturity in only 10 to 12 weeks, and makes a reliable cover crop in summer to fit a small warm-season slot. This hardy plant grows well even in high altitudes and northern latitudes. In my experience, no insect pests or diseases seem to attack it.

Harvesting. When the plants have completed their cycle, the seeds will appear dry and brown. At that point, they are easily stripped into a bucket or other container.

Not all seeds ripen at once, so a good rule of thumb is to harvest when 75 percent of the seeds are ripe enough to be easily stripped from the plants, and then to harvest the rest a few weeks later.

Allow the seeds to completely dry by spreading them on trays in a warm, protected place and stirring them once or twice a day for three days. Their colour will become dark brown or black, and your fingernail won't be able to make an indentation when they are ready to store.

Yields. If you harvest each plant twice in this way, you can figure on obtaining 3 to 4 pounds (1.4 to 1.8 kg) of seed from a growing area 10 by 10 feet (3 by 3 m).

Saving Seed. Your buckwheat seed is ready to be planted as another cover crop in your garden or to be used to grow buckwheat "lettuce" microgreens. (See page 95.)

Above: Buckwheat is a marvellous cover crop but cannot tolerate any frost. Karen Mouat photo

Above left: Buckwheat is delicious in pancakes and many other baked goods. For a tasty and versatile appetizer, try Buckwheat Blini with Savoury Toppings (page 120). *Photo courtesy Darren Muir/Stocksy.*
Above right: Buckwheat is a versatile, gluten-free crop that's rich in protein, fibre and carbo-hydrates. *Photo courtesy Oleg_Ermak/Thinkstock*

HOW TO ENJOY BUCKWHEAT GROATS

My history with buckwheat predates my gardening life. Even when I was a teenager, buckwheat pancakes were my favourite. Pancakes made with flour ground from buckwheat's groats are light, foamy, rich and earthy. They are even more of a treat when topped with buckwheat honey. Dark and strongly fragrant, it makes for a unique and most delightful experience.

In addition to those memorable pancakes, there are many other simple ways to savour the nourishment of buckwheat groats and flour.

In Baking. While buckwheat's starchy endosperm is white and makes up most of its flour, bits of the hull can sometimes be seen in the flour as dark specks. Dark buckwheat flour is also known as *farine de sarrasin.* Combine it with whole-wheat or non-gluten flour to make wonderful breads, pancakes, cakes and muffins.

Toasted or Roasted. Buckwheat groats can be found in health food stores whole or crushed, roasted or unroasted. Roasting or toasting gives them a grilled flavour and makes the buckwheat less moist and chewy, similar to the difference between toast and bread.

It's easy to roast groats yourself: simply put them into a 300F (150C) oven in an uncovered, unoiled pan for a few minutes. Keep an eye on them, stirring the groats around a bit as needed, to ensure that they don't burn.

Or toast them. Heat a large unoiled skillet on medium heat. Pour groats into it so they just cover the bottom; do not layer them. Toast, stirring continually with a wooden spatula to prevent burning, for 2 to 4 minutes or until golden brown. Repeat with additional batches.

As Hot Cereal. Cook up a pot of buckwheat groats as a hearty breakfast. The formula for cooking buckwheat cereal is simple: 2 cups (475 mL) water to 1 cup (250 mL) groats, heated to a boil and simmered for 20 minutes. Toasted buckwheat, or kasha, requires a little less water and only 15 minutes of cooking. The flavour of both is earthy and satisfying.

In a Simple Supper. On its own, buckwheat has a richer flavour than rice or other grains, yet doesn't feel heavy on the digestive system. Because it is a complete protein, buckwheat makes for a pleasing meal in these very simple ways:

1. Add cooked buckwheat groats to soups, to give them deeper flavour and added texture.
2. Add a few Styrian pumpkin seeds, fresh peas, chopped chives and scallions to cooked and cooled buckwheat groats, for a delicious lunch or dinner salad. Splash on a bit of your favourite dressing, along with a dash of salt or seasonings.
3. Use cooked buckwheat groats in stir-fries with carrots, mushrooms, tomatoes, celery and onions. Toss in some chopped garden greens, including a few buckwheat leaves, in the last few minutes of cooking. Season to taste.

CHAPTER 6

Flaxseed

Early in my career as a seedsman trying to encourage self-reliance, I realized it was difficult to find crops that could provide an ample amount of oil to one's diet. Soybeans and sunflowers seemed to be good options, but flaxseed (*Linum usitatissimum*) looked even better when I discovered how easy it was to grow and eat.

FROM FABRIC TO FOOD

When I read up on it, I was convinced that flax had a lot to offer. In fact, it seemed to have as long a history and to be regarded with as much esteem as the other superfoods in this book.

There is some evidence that flax cultivation may have started over ten thousand years ago, becoming common in regions of the Middle East around 3000 BC or earlier. From the very beginning, the value of flax was both culinary and domestic, since flax fibres could be spun into linen to provide clothing and other textile-related products.

Most commercial flax production now involves oilseed varieties of flax, whose seeds are dried and crushed to produce different grades of oil. In addition to culinary oil, non-food-grade flaxseed and linseed oil are produced for wood finishes, paints and other industrial coatings. Food-grade flaxseed or linseed meal or oil can also be used in livestock feed. Canada is the world's largest producer of oilseed flax, followed by Russia, France and Argentina.

Opposite: You might want to plant flax just for its flowers. *Karen Mouat photo*

NUTRIENT-DENSE

I say it's time for unprocessed flaxseed to be considered a uniquely nourishing food in its own right! Flaxseed is one of the most nutrient-dense foods available and is especially high in fibre, protein, thiamine, manganese, magnesium, phosphorus and selenium. It also has good amounts of zinc, copper, iron, potassium and vitamin B$_6$.[38]

OMEGA-3 AND ANTI-AGING LIGNANS

Flaxseed is the richest source of alpha-linolenic acid, a plant-based omega-3 fatty acid often referred to as ALA.[39] The ALA in flaxseed helps to protect the lining of the digestive tract, and has been shown to be beneficial for people suffering from Crohn's disease and other digestive ailments.[40] It also helps to reduce dryness and flakiness of the skin and hair, and can lessen the symptoms of acne, rosacea and eczema.[41]

Flaxseed is packed with polyphenols,[42] called lignans, that have antioxidant benefits for anti-aging, hormone balance and cellular health.[43] Lignans support the growth of probiotics in the gut and are known for their anti-viral properties.[44] Among all commonly eaten foods, researchers now rank flaxseed as the number-one source of lignans.[45] Flaxseed contains an estimated seven times more lignans than its closest runner-up, sesame seed.[46]

In addition to all this, studies have shown that flaxseed may be beneficial in fighting breast and prostate,[47] ovarian, lung and colon[48] cancers.[49] Flaxseed is also recommended for heart health,[50] with Health Canada linking it to a reduction in blood cholesterol.[51]

NON-GLUTEN FIBRE

The large amounts of soluble and insoluble fibre in flaxseed support colon health, reduce sugar cravings and help to lower cholesterol.[52] Together with the omega-3 fatty acid, the fibre helps you feel satisfied longer, so you will eat fewer calories overall.[53]

Flaxseed is great for people with celiac disease or gluten sensitivities,[54] replacing gluten-containing inflammatory grains with anti-inflammatory properties.

A CARPET OF BLUE

Even with flaxseed's impressive nutritional and health benefits, what sparked my love of flax were my experiences with growing it in my food gardens. It is so easy to grow, and does well with various planting times and in a wide range of soils. What's more, flax is a tough and beautiful plant that never has any disease or pest problems.

I love the way its delicate blue flowers fall to the ground in mid-afternoon to form a carpet of blue, and how a whole new batch of blueness appears atop the plants the next day. I love seeing the luminous golden seeds on trays in the greenhouse after I've threshed the small globular seed capsules, and how they feel like liquid gold when I run them through my fingers.

Varieties. I've been so smitten by the Golden flax cultivar I first grew in 1988 that, unlike the other crops described in this book, I've done almost no trialling of other varieties. Not only are

Above: The cycle of flax flower to seed is a joy to observe. Dan Jason photo

Above left: These Golden flaxseeds are oozing their wonderful oil. *Dan Jason photo. Above right:* Each round flaxseed capsule contains up to six seeds. *Karen Mouat photo*

Golden seeds easy to grow, they are chewable and delicious eaten right out of your hand.

Soil and Sun. I've grown flax successfully in such a variety of conditions that I recommend growing it no matter what your soil type. Give it as sunny a spot as possible.

Planting Time. I've planted flax as early as the beginning of April and as late as early July. Early and late plantings have been equally successful for me, and I've been extremely impressed by flax's adaptability to different weather conditions. It takes between 90 and 100 days to mature.

Sowing. Sow flaxseed about ½ inch (1.25 cm) deep and 1 to 2 inches (2.5 to 5 cm) apart, in rows 6 to 12 inches (15 to 30 cm) apart. The plants will be visible in about a week.

Strong, robust plants grow to about 30 inches (76 cm) high and flower for about three weeks. Each flower lasts for only a day, but for those three weeks it's a surprise and delight to see more pretty blue blossoms appear almost magically each morning, only to fall and carpet the ground again each afternoon.

Maintenance. Flax plants require little maintenance beyond customary weeding. They do not have to be thinned. Watering will not usually be necessary, unless in the case of extreme drought, and no problems with pests or diseases are to be expected.

Harvesting. After flowering, the flax forms round seed heads that shift from a soft green to a papery brown. There are about thirty capsules per stalk, each with five or six seeds. It is very easy to strip these upward and off into a bucket or tub when they are dry.

Threshing. Flaxseed can then be dried further on trays, then walked on or squeezed by hand to release the seeds from their hulls. The chaff can be screened and/or blown away.

Yields. A small area planted with flax can supply a healthy sprinkling of flax for many bowls of granola and many snacks. You should easily harvest 5 pounds (2.3 kg) of flax from a patch of 10 rows that are each 10 feet (3 m) long.

Saving Seed. As with all the other grains and seeds in this book, saving seeds for next year's planting is simply a matter of not eating all the harvest!

HOW TO ENJOY FLAXSEED

Health advocates often promote consuming flaxseed in ground form, based on the belief that our bodies cannot fully access the nutrients of flaxseed eaten whole. At home, a coffee grinder works well for this purpose. (Store flaxseed in the refrigerator or freezer after grinding.) Using flaxseed in soaked or sprouted form is also a popular way to increase its absorption. (See pages 89–92.) I think chewing it as a snack works well too.

However you choose to eat it, there are many ways to add flaxseed to your daily diet:

1. Toss it into smoothies.
2. Stir it into yogurt.
3. Add it to granola or to any cold or cooked breakfast cereal.
4. Sprinkle it over salads.
5. Shake it into a stir-fry.
6. Add it to homemade muffins, breads, cookies or pancakes. The ALA in flaxseed has been found to be stable at oven temperatures of 300F (150C) for at least 3 hours of baking, which means that it retains its health benefits when cooked at a medium or low temperature.[55]
7. Or eat flaxseed my favourite way: as a satisfying, chewable snack! With no shells or hulls, flaxseed has an oily and crunchy texture with a slightly spicy flavour and is fun to munch.

CHAPTER 7

Styrian Pumpkin Seeds

In the early '80s, I discovered and pursued hulless pumpkin seeds. I found them to be a wonderful, high-yielding, protein-rich food that can easily be grown in temperate gardens.

EASY EATING

Like hulless barleys and wheats, hulless pumpkin seeds don't need to go through a difficult shelling process. The seed is encased in a thin membrane that may be consumed along with the seed. The seeds can be lightly toasted with a little salt or, like flaxseed, eaten raw. I find them delicious. They are a convenient protein source and a great snack or addition to smoothies or salads.

STANDOUT SQUASH

I trialled quite a few pumpkin varieties that had hulless seeds before I found Styrian pumpkin (*Cucurbita pepo* var. *styriaca*), which really stood out for its rich taste, earliness of appearance and productivity. Now this is the only one I grow. That's not to say there is not a diversity of hulless pumpkin seeds to pursue. But, as with Golden flaxseed, I decided to stick with my favourite variety. It's enough for me that I'm maintaining hundreds of cultivars of beans, grains, greens, tomatoes, lettuces and herbs!

Opposite: Styrian pumpkin is my favourite variety, producing rich-tasting hulless seeds. Photo courtesy Dora Zett/Shutterstock

Above left: Striking, brightly coloured Styrian pumpkin flowers. Photo courtesy Uebersbach8362/Wikimedia Commons. Above right: Pumpkin seeds make a delicious snack and are great for maintaining a healthy heart. Photo courtesy Riverlim/ Thinkstock

ANCIENT ORIGIN

Squash was first domesticated in Central and South America eight to ten thousand years ago. Styrian pumpkins are a new twist on an ancient theme, with the earliest confirmed record of oil pumpkin seeds, in the Styria region of Austria, dating back to 1697.[56] Their oil is now an important export commodity of Austria and Slovenia; it is made by pressing roasted hulless Styrian pumpkin seeds.

A HANDFUL FOR HEALTH

Styrian pumpkin seeds have long been enjoyed as a nourishing snack, especially in Mediterranean countries, and are credited with easing and preventing bladder and prostate problems.[57] Another reason for their being so valuable today is that their antioxidant properties are higher than those of any other variety of pumpkin.[58]

Indeed, Styrian pumpkin seeds have made North American news in recent years because of their power in protecting prostate health. Studies now show that prostate enlargement may be slowed, stopped and even reversed.[59] Styrian pumpkin seeds are a great source of zinc, phosphorus, magnesium and essential fatty acids—while most men suffering from prostate enlargement are deficient in these nutrients.

Studies have also shown that pumpkin seeds may lower the risk of kidney stones,[60] reduce hypertension,[61] relieve insomnia

and anxiety (thanks to their high levels of tryptophan),[62] and eliminate parasites.[63]

Containing 50 percent linoleic acid (omega-6), one of the essential polyunsaturated fatty acids necessary for maintaining health, along with carotenoids and phytosterols—and no cholesterol—Styrian pumpkin seeds are an ideal nutrient for heart and circulatory health.[64] They are also credited for reducing hair loss, helping to prevent diabetes, soothing an overactive bladder and reducing inflammation in the body.[65]

The vitamin-E content in Styrian pumpkin seeds is five times that of olive oil. They also are rich in vitamins A, thiamine, riboflavin, niacin, B_6 and K. As well as having a high content of manganese, phosphorus and zinc, they are a good source of magnesium, copper, iron and protein.[66]

And with the seeds so easy to eat, all you need to do is munch a delicious handful every other day to help maintain good health.

PROLIFIC IN THE GARDEN

The Styrian pumpkin plant is problem free, fast growing and a rewardingly prolific producer of large fruits. I have found it to be one of the easiest squashes to grow successfully.

Varieties. Styrian pumpkins have mottled, subdued green stripes on a pale yellow-orange background with darker orange areas. They grow to be about 12 inches (30 cm) wide.

Above: The green stripes are particularly clear on this Styrian pumpkin. *Photo courtesy Claus Rebler/Wikimedia Commons*

Soil and Sun. Squashes are heavy feeders. In a crop rotation, they are best grown after a green manure or an application of compost. Too much nitrogen in the soil will produce leafy growth at the expense of the fruit. The sunnier the spot you choose for Styrian pumpkin, the better.

Planting Time. I have had very good results sowing seeds directly in the ground once the soil has warmed up, around late May. However, Styrian pumpkins are large plants with vines up to 10 ft (3 m) long, so starting the plants in 4-inch (10-cm) pots in early May is a more practical approach.

Sowing. Wait to transplant the pumpkins until the roots are just starting to come through the holes in the bottoms of their containers. Then you can plant the babies to their final distance apart, about 3 feet (0.9 m). They also can be planted in hills, with 3 plants per hill.

Maintenance. I usually mulch my plants heavily after it has really warmed up in June. Until then, I weed by hand or with a hoe, so that the earth and young plants can be warmed by the sun's rays. Vines usually become self-mulching by July, in any case.

It's good to have lots of pollinator plants (like buckwheat) around. Pollination by insects is required for pumpkin's seed production. The more visits by pollinators, the greater the fruit set, fruit size and weight, and number of seeds.

The plants do well even in cool, damp summers, and I'm usually able to harvest my Styrian pumpkin seeds by mid- to late September.

Harvesting. Harvest the pumpkins after they go from green to striped orange/green, or after the first frost. Fully mature fruit have seeds with greater oil content than those from immature fruit.

Remove the seeds at harvest. I have found that the easiest way to open the pumpkins is with a small hatchet. After I have removed all the seeds, I rinse them with cold water and remove any stringy parts of the flesh. Then I spread them out on screens to dry, stirring several times a day, for three or four days.

Yields. Each plant grows about four to six pumpkins, and you can easily get a pound (0.45 kg) of seeds per plant.

Saving Seed. Styrian pumpkins are the only crop discussed in this book for which the possible crossing of seeds is an important consideration. Styrian pumpkin is a member of the *Cucurbita pepo* family and will cross with other cultivars in the same family, including other pumpkin varieties and acorn, scallop, crookneck, zucchini, delicata and spaghetti squashes. Bees could cross-fertilize any of these if they are within a quarter mile of each other—so it's best to grow only Styrian pumpkin in order to keep the seed true.

HOW TO ENJOY STYRIAN PUMPKIN SEEDS

There are so many ways to enjoy the amazing benefits of Styrian pumpkin seeds.

From Raw to Roasted. Try eating Styrian pumpkin seeds in all of these easy ways:

1. Raw is considered by many health advocates to be among the healthiest ways to consume pumpkin seeds.
2. Soaking the seeds may be even better, as this helps to awaken their vitality by releasing phytonutrients. (See pages 90–92.)
3. Some people find dehydrated seeds more palatable. You can dry them yourself in a dehydrator or oven.
4. Lightly pan-toasted pumpkin seeds are particularly flavourful thrown onto salads or stir-fries. Stir the seeds steadily with a wooden spoon on medium heat for a minute or two. Avoid getting distracted, or your seeds may scorch.
5. Pumpkin seeds are also nice when roasted for no more than 20 minutes—preferably at a lower temperature of about 170F/80C, to safeguard the integrity of the nutrients.[67]
6. Simmered then roasted is perhaps the tastiest way to enjoy tender yet crunchy pumpkin seeds. Add ½ cup (120 mL) seed to 2 cups (475 mL) boiling, salted (2 teaspoons/10 mL) water. Simmer 10 minutes. Roast as described above.

And the Rest of the Pumpkin? Commercially, Styrian pumpkin flesh is not used for human food; it generally is composted, or fed to animals. The vegetable part of this fruit was never favoured over pumpkin varieties that produce more and better pulp. But you don't need to waste this nourishing food! I have found it tasty and good enough to be used in pies, breads, soups and other recipes requiring pumpkin.

CHAPTER 8

Quinoa

I first started growing quinoa (*Chenopodium quinoa*) in 1985, when it was virtually unknown in Canada. A quarter of a century later, in 2010, this seed rose to popularity along with a cookbook called *Quinoa 365: The Everyday Superfood,*[68] which was on the bestseller list for months on end.

"MOTHER GRAIN" OF THE INCAS

Long before that book hit the shelves, I was intrigued by this "mother grain" of the Incas grown and revered five thousand years ago. In the harsh conditions of their home in the towering altiplano of Peru and Bolivia, with altitudes as high as 12,300 feet (3,750 m), quinoa grew well and provided the sustenance required to endure at such elevations. Like the barley crops of Tibetans in the Himalayas, quinoa, along with some animal oils, provided the Incas with their main source of nutrition and energy.[69]

In the 1500s, the conquering Spanish recognized the importance of quinoa to the Incas and made it illegal to cultivate, consume or worship this plant. From then on, quinoa cultivation was greatly reduced and was relegated to hidden, higher-altitude areas. Nowadays, this ancient seed is a secret no longer, and is grown in many South American countries as well as in Europe, Asia and North America.

Opposite: Quinoa is a popular superfood, rich in protein, amino acids, vitamins and minerals. *Karen Mouat photo*

A RAIN CHECK

Years ago, I obtained quinoa from David Cusack, of the Quinoa Corporation in Colorado, who had brought some from the high mountains of Bolivia. There was some doubt as to whether the strains I obtained would work near sea level in the Pacific Northwest; nevertheless, I had a successful first crop. It was easy to multiply seed because one quinoa plant produced an ounce of sesame-sized seeds.

It wasn't until the third year that I realized how lucky I had been with my first two seed harvests. A friend came from Vancouver Island to see what quinoa looked like at harvest time. When I excitedly pointed out the plants to him, we were both aghast at what looked like thousands of maggots covering their tops. Looking more closely, we saw that, actually, the seeds simply had sprouted on the plants. I remembered that it had rained heavily the night before. Thus I learned that, because quinoa is so adapted to the very dry conditions of the high mountains of Bolivia and Peru, you'd better have a plan in case it rains at harvest time.

Since then, I've kept a close watch on my quinoa in September. If it threatens to rain when the quinoa leaves have fallen and the clusters of seeds are drying, I cut the plants near the base and bring them under cover to ensure the harvesting of dry seeds.

BITTER SEED

When I started cooking with quinoa, I found another concern. The seed is coated with saponins, bitter-tasting phytochemicals that deter birds and deer from harvesting the seeds before you do. Named after *sapo*, Latin for "soap," saponins produce a lather when mixed with water. This doesn't make for a very pleasant eating experience, unless your quinoa is rinsed very well before cooking.

Rinsing it in cool water, in a blender at low speed, helped somewhat, but I had to repeat this process at least three times before the water stopped frothing up with saponins. What worked better was putting quinoa in old stockings and running them through the rinse cycle of my washing machine!

With these two drawbacks—quinoa's susceptibility to moisture at harvest, and its bitter seed coat—I doubted that it would ever become popular as a major food crop in North America. I felt that amaranth was a much more likely candidate to become the next superfood. How wrong I was!

In the 1980s and '90s, the quinoa that was available in supermarkets and health food stores had some of the saponins removed but still had to be thoroughly rinsed. Nowadays, though, store-bought quinoa is quite good, and hardly needs rinsing because effective mechanical rubbing processes have been developed. However, that doesn't solve the problem for gardeners growing their own quinoa.

No doubt, there will one day be varieties that don't have a lot of saponins on the seed, and there will be cultivars that resist sprouting on the plant. I've tried to warn seed customers that quinoa isn't such an easy crop to grow. That hasn't stopped quinoa from being one of my top-selling seed packets every year.

SUPERFOOD SENSATION

It's no wonder that quinoa has caught on as a superfood and that so many people want to try growing it. Quinoa contains about 16 percent protein[70] with an abundance of all nine essential amino acids,[71] and is rich in vitamins E, B_6, thiamine, riboflavin and folate, as well as potassium, zinc, copper, magnesium, manganese and phosphorus.[72] It is higher in calcium and iron than rice, wheat or corn.[73]

Easy to digest, it has good flavour with a simple, distinctive taste that allows great versatility for cooking purposes. It can be substituted for other grains in many recipes, and is much more filling. Not a true cereal grain, quinoa is gluten-free[74] and can be eaten by people who suffer from grain allergies.

With all the essential amino acids necessary for human growth and development, quinoa is a complete protein that contains absolutely no cholesterol or trans fat. Its ratio of protein to carbohydrate is exceptional, with the germ making up 60 percent of the grain.[75] It is also an excellent source of fibre and can help to regulate blood sugar.[76]

Quinoa is high in histidine and a source of arginine—amino acids essential for infants and young children[77]—and contains lysine, which is lacking in most cereals.[78] And it is a powerhouse source of the antioxidant flavonoids quercetin and kaempferol,

Above left: The hues of Multi-hued quinoa emit a special energy when you're amidst them. *Dan Jason photo. Above right:* This quinoa has many hues on the same flower. *Karen Mouat photo*

which have anti-diabetes,[79] anti-inflammatory, anti-viral and anti-cancer properties.[80]

GO FOR THE GREENS

Like amaranth and buckwheat, quinoa is a leafy pseudocereal. Picking up to five leaves at a time off your quinoa plant won't hurt it, and the young greens make tasty salad material that is high in phytonutrients, vitamins and minerals.[81] Carrots juiced with a small amount of quinoa leaves make an invigorating drink. Older greens can be steamed, stir-fried, or incorporated into curries or casseroles.

GRAND IN THE GARDEN

Most cultivars of quinoa grow 4 to 8 feet (120 to 250 cm) high and, when in flower, are majestic plants that lend radiance to any garden. Their unique flower hues are most striking at a close distance, around dawn or dusk.

Varieties. Named varieties of quinoa are increasingly available from seed companies. Most North Americans would be hard-pressed to describe the subtle differences in flavour between cultivars. That said, my Black quinoa has an earthier flavour and a crunchier texture than others, and even seems to resist sprouting in wet conditions.

My own Multi-hued quinoa is a result of selections I've made from the quinoa I obtained thirty years ago. I've tended to select not only for the health of the plants but also for diversity of flower colour. As with the other crops in this book, there is tremendous diversity waiting to be discovered and appreciated. I have heard of quinoa seeds that are ivory, magenta, yellow, orange, red or green.

Soil and Sun. Quinoa thrives in rich, well-drained loam but is quite adaptable, disease-free and drought-tolerant. I have grown it successfully in many different conditions including sandy, loamy and peaty soils, in both wet and dry seasons. Plants grown in average garden soil will be 4 to 6 feet (120 to 180 cm) tall, while those grown in very fertile soil may surpass 8 feet (250 cm).

While quinoa grows well in both full-sun and partly shaded areas, it should have at least six hours of sun a day. Given its sensitivity to rain, try growing quinoa under the eaves of the south side of your home, if space allows!

Planting Times. Quinoa grows best where maximum temperatures do not exceed 90F (32C) and nighttime temperatures are cool. For most southern Canadian and northern US sites, the best time to plant quinoa is late April to late May. When soil temperatures are around 60F (16C), seedlings emerge within three to four days. However, when quinoa seeds are planted in soil with night temperatures much above that, they may not germinate. In that case, it's best to refrigerate the seeds before planting.

Sowing. Quinoa will germinate more successfully with a finely prepared surface and adequate moisture. Seeds should be sown no more than ¼ inch (0.6 cm) deep. Rows are best 18 to 24 inches (46 to 61 cm) apart. Planting can be done either by hand or with a row seeder.

As quinoa resembles lamb's quarters, especially in the early stages of growth, it is best to sow seed in rows to avoid any

Above left: When it flowers, Multi-hued quinoa has has a broad range of flower colours. *Above right:* These quinoa are just starting to dry down. *Both photos by Dan Jason*

confusion when weeding. (Later, it is easier to tell these two apart because of lamb's quarters' habit of more branching.)

Since quinoa seed is small, you can avoid considerable thinning by mixing it with sand before sowing. Plants should eventually be thinned 6 to 18 inches (15 to 46 cm) apart. Thinnings make great additions to salad!

Maintenance. Soil moisture is probably sufficient for germinating the seed until early June. Given good soil moisture, don't water the plants until they reach the two- or three-leaf stage. While quinoa is a low-maintenance crop, weeds should be discouraged by cultivation or mulching, particularly when the plants are just in the beginning stages.

Quinoa may appear slow-growing at first, but it is extremely drought-tolerant. As the plants reach about 12 inches (30 cm) in height, they start to grow very rapidly, with the canopy filling in to shade out weeds and to reduce moisture loss through evaporation. As I write this in the heat of summer, I have a beautiful stand of quinoa that has never been watered or rained on.

You may have noticed pigweed or lamb's quarters flower heads occasionally being munched by insect larvae; the same is sometimes true of cultivated quinoa. This shouldn't have any serious impact upon the harvest.

Harvesting. Quinoa is ready to harvest when the leaves have fallen, leaving just dried seed heads. Quinoa resists light frosts, especially if the soil is dry. As long as maturing seed is past the green stage, frost will cause little damage, and harvesting can be done a day or two later.

It is important to watch the weather when quinoa is ready to be harvested. As I've noted, the dry seed may germinate if rained on. If you choose to bring the plants under cover because of possible rain, you'll find that they take up surprisingly little space when stood up in a corner of a greenhouse or indoor room.

If the heads are not completely dry, harvest them when you can barely indent the seeds with your thumbnail. Seeds can be easily stripped upward off the stalk with a gloved hand.

After harvesting, it is important to dry your crop further, to ensure that it won't mould in storage. Spread it out on trays in the hot sun or near an indoor heat source for three to four days. Stir occasionally, until the seeds are as dry as possible.

Threshing. Quinoa can be cleaned with screens, by winnowing, or with a fan or other blowing device. Quinoa has no hulls to remove.

Yields. An ounce or so of seed per plant is common, but you can easily get more than 6 ounces (170 grams) per plant if grown in your best soil.

Normal commercial yields for quinoa are 1,200 to 2,000 pounds (544–907 kg) per acre. For commercially grown quinoa, agricultural combines are still being adapted to the lightness of the seed, and full harvest potential is yet to be realized. Much better results are obtained from labour-intensive harvesting; yields of more than 5,000 pounds (2,268 kg) per acre have been reported in Central and South America.

Saving Seed. Quinoa can cross with its wild relative, lamb's quarters or pigweed (*Chenopodium album*), so it's best to keep your garden free of that weed—especially as pigweed is capable of flowering and going to seed at any stage of its growth.

It's also possible for quinoa to cross with other quinoa varieties. To be safe, grow only one kind, or separate cultivars by as much distance as you can to keep your variety true. Don't worry too much about this, though; I've experimented with growing differ-ent varieties side by side and have not had any crosses. Even if I did have one, I wouldn't assume that it was inferior; crosses can sometimes result in interesting new possibilities!

HOW TO ENJOY QUINOA SEED

When planning to eat quinoa, keep in mind the bitter saponin (which deters birds and deer from harvesting the seeds before you do). Because of this coating, quinoa requires thorough rinsing before cooking, as already discussed. You can get away with less rinsing by mixing quinoa with other grains or pulses, which render the saponins hardly noticeable. What's left is believed to help in lowering cholesterol, boosting the immune system and reducing the risk of cancer.[82]

Cold or hot, quinoa can mean breakfast, lunch or dinner in the quickest and most nourishing ways.

As Hot Cereal. Bring equal volumes of quinoa and water to a boil, reduce to a simmer, cover and cook 12 to 15 minutes, until all water is absorbed. For a more porridge-like consistency, use a larger proportion of water.

With Fruit. Cook quinoa with chopped apples, raisins and cinnamon for a great hot or cold breakfast cereal.

As a Side Dish or Lunch. A simple yet sustaining meal can be prepared by adding chopped and briefly sautéed carrots, scallions or celery to cooked quinoa, along with a bit of butter or oil.

Greek Style. For a cold Greek salad, try mixing 1 cup (250 mL) cooked and cooled quinoa with ½ cup (120 mL) each of pitted olives, diced chopped leeks or green onions, crumbled feta cheese and finely chopped red pepper. Add oregano to taste, thoroughly mix, and chill before serving.

Four Meals for Four. Let quinoa be your fast-food fix when you need a quick dinner or lunch.

1. Quinoa Curry: In ¼ cup (60 mL) oil, cook a chopped onion with 1 teaspoon (5 mL) of ginger and a finely chopped clove of garlic on medium heat, until the onion softens. Stir in 1 teaspoon (5 mL) powdered ginger, 1 tablespoon (15 mL) curry powder, ½ teaspoon (2.5 mL) each salt and ground coriander, ¼ teaspoon (1 mL) each turmeric and cumin, plus 1 pinch cayenne. Cook for 1 minute, then add 1 cup (250 mL) fresh peas and 1¼ cups (300 mL) vegetable broth. Cover and simmer for 5 minutes. Add 1 cup (250 mL) quinoa, return to boiling,

cover and simmer for another 12 minutes or until liquid is absorbed.

2. Quinoa with Swedish Brown, Black Turtle or Pinquito Beans: Sauté ½ cup (120 mL) chopped onion and pepper in 1 tablespoon (15 mL) oil, until softened. Add and stir in 1 cup (250 mL) water and bring to a boil. Stir in 1 cup (250 mL) cooked beans, then 1 cup (250 mL) cooked quinoa. Cover and simmer for 10 minutes. Remove from heat and stir in a handful of chopped cilantro and ¼ teaspoon (1 mL) cayenne or chili pepper.

3. Quinoa with Baked Squash: In a large skillet, cook 2 cups (475 mL) cubed squash in 2 tablespoons (30 mL) oil over medium-high heat until soft. Stir in 2 cups (475 mL) cooked quinoa and 2 cups (475 mL) grated cheddar cheese. Place in a greased casserole and bake in a medium oven for 30 minutes.

4. Quinoa Citrus Salad: This wonderful salad calls for 2 cups (475 mL) cooked and cooled quinoa. In a large bowl, toss quinoa with ½ cup (120 mL) chopped red pepper, ½ cup (120 mL) slivered almonds and ⅓ cup (80 mL) chopped sweet onion. In a small bowl, stir together 1 tablespoon (15 mL) olive oil, 3 tablespoons (45 mL) orange juice and 1 teaspoon (5 mL) each of cider vinegar and honey. Pour dressing over salad and toss until well combined. Line 4 bowls with lettuce leaves, add sections from 2 oranges and then top with salad.

Above left, clockwise from top: Multi-hued quinoa, Cahuil quinoa, Black quinoa. *Above right:* Quinoa and Amaranth Salad with Roasted Root Vegetables, Green Onions and Blood Orange (page 138) is just one of many delicious ways to prepare quinoa.

CHAPTER 9

Soybeans

When I was researching high-protein crops in the mid-1980s, soybeans (*Glycine max*) really caught my attention because they had twice as much protein as other beans. They also have such a significant oil content that they are considered an oilseed and not a pulse crop by the Food and Agriculture Organization of the United Nations (UN).

At the time of my research, the soybeans obtainable in health food stores seemed to be of only one variety. Unfortunately, that light yellow cultivar was practically indigestible—even when soaked for days and cooked for many hours. It had a tinny off-taste that seemed to deplete me instead of giving nourishment. I surmised that the variety was the same one fed to animals across North America.

MY SOYBEAN SEARCH

My pursuit took a much more positive turn, though, when I discovered that Johnny's Selected Seeds in Maine had a black-seeded cultivar called Black Jet. I was very impressed by how easily grown and delectable it was. Black Jet yielded well and cooked up in about ninety minutes after an overnight soaking. Not only was this soybean very tasty, but its richness meant that a little went a long way toward making me feel full and satisfied. A small side dish of cooked soybeans made it easy to create a very complete meal.

Opposite: When soybeans have plumped their pods, they are ready to be eaten as edamame. Photo courtesy Alan Shapiro/Stocksy

Above: Soybeans grow more lushly in soil where they've grown before.
Karen Mouat photo

I obtained a few more varieties from the Seed Savers Exchange, as well as one from Grand Forks, British Columbia. Hokkaido Black was a shiny black soybean, unlike the slate-like dullness of Black Jet seeds. Manitoba Brown had a rich earthy tone. Shirofumi was a large green seed. The Doukhobor heirloom Grand Forks seeds were a two-tone gold and brown that looked like kids' candies, and Agate was a smaller version of Grand Forks.

All these varieties have grown well for me, and are sweet, rich and buttery when cooked like a regular bean. They also serve as excellent edamame beans, a term used for soybeans that have been simmered for four to five minutes, or steamed for ten, while in fully ripe pods that have not yet dried down.

STELLAR SOURCE OF WHOLE FOOD

The more I learned about soybeans, the more puzzled I became that we processed this wonderful legume in every imaginable fashion—such as for soy sauce, tempeh, miso and tofu—instead of simply cooking it. I couldn't understand why the gardening world didn't recognize soybeans as a valuable grow-your-own food crop.

Soybeans have so very much to offer. They have no cholesterol, and are extremely low in saturated fats and sodium. They are an excellent source of dietary fibre and are high in iron, calcium, molybdenum, copper, manganese, zinc, phosphorus, potassium, magnesium, riboflavin, vitamin K and omega-3 fatty acids.[83]

Perhaps even more exciting is the fact that soybeans are the only legume containing all nine essential amino acids.[84] Soybeans contain over 35 percent protein by weight, with the World Health Organization giving them the highest possible score for food value.[85] The amino acids, or building blocks, in soybeans are in just the right ratio to support good health, and a ¾-cup (180-mL) serving of cooked soybeans equals the amount of protein found in ½ cup (120 mL) of meat.[86]

THE BIG QUESTION

In fact, an acre of soybeans produces at least fifteen times more useable protein than an equivalent acre used to graze beef cattle.[87] The carbon output created by raising beef is more than thirty times the output that results from growing an equal serving of soybeans.[88]

Ironically, vast acreages of soybeans have been grown to feed animals, and these heavily subsidized meat and dairy industries have wreaked ecological havoc on water and soil resources. So, my question was: Why grow soybeans to feed animals that are used to feed people, when we could be growing soybeans to eat directly?

My answer was that I was going to do my best to wake people up to the potential of soybeans. Soybeans were listed in my first Salt Spring Seeds catalogue in 1986, and I've never looked back.

I've been offering several varieties of soybeans for three decades and have never had a crop failure with them. Soybeans still haven't sufficiently caught on, however, either as a special garden crop or as a bean to be incorporated into a healthy diet.

SO WHAT WENT WRONG?

What happened instead was the introduction of the Roundup Ready Soybean.

In the mid-'90s, I started receiving glossy promotional material from the Canadian government, lauding the benefits and wonders of bioengineered food crops and the importance of Canada's leaping into biotechnology ahead of other countries. Especially highlighted was a genetically modified soybean created by Monsanto Company to withstand applications of the bestselling herbicide, glyphosate, to which they gave their patented name "Roundup."[89]

I was extremely doubtful that this prolific manufacturer of poisons[90] would promote a product that would contribute to the health of the planet. To my mind, there was a qualitative difference between the original soybean and a GMO soybean with extra genes inserted to render it immune from a herbicide that basically kills any green living thing.

My apprehensions have only increased as I've watched the percentage of GMO soybeans cultivated in North America skyrocket from 17 percent in 1996 to include most of those grown today.[91] Many studies have shown the dangers of GMO foods (see *GMO Myths and Truths* for the best summation of these[92]), but the powerful biotech lobby continues to promote them as safe and benign.

I chose to leave the farm I was renting in 2001 because the owner starting spraying Roundup on his grape plantation above my gardens. I'll never forget the deathly look of the land afterwards.

It has now become common practice in North America to aerial-spray glyphosate on both non-GMO and GMO crops, including wheat, canola and flax. This is often done just a few days before harvest, to kill any vegetation and to make combining easy.[93] We are told that there are no poison residues on the foods sprayed days before they are gathered for our tables, although experts, researchers and policy-makers from the World Health Organization have expressed concerns to the contrary.[94]

These days, some form of Roundup Ready soybean is found in a large percentage of processed supermarket foods.[95] I'm still asking why we don't eat unmodified, unadulterated, unprocessed soybeans, one of the best whole foods in existence.

AN ANCIENT STAPLE CROP

I've been glad to maintain some fine soybean varieties because they are exceptional as basic, nourishing food. That pleasure is now tempered by necessity; the realization that Salt Spring Seeds is one of the few remaining sources of unmodified seed is a most sobering one. Even Johnny's Selected Seeds no longer carries Black Jet.

Soybeans have been an important staple in East Asia since ancient times and are now also a major crop in Brazil, Argentina, China, India, Africa and North America.

Yet in North America, more than five billion bushels of soybeans are harvested annually, with virtually none intended for direct human consumption. If soybeans are ever to catch on as beans that can be eaten and appreciated like pinto or kidney beans, it seems to me that people who grow their own will be the ones to start this trend and to create the demand.

Above: Soybeans should be planted when the weather is warm: late May or early June in southern Canada or the northern US. *Photo courtesy Darcy Maulsby/ Thinkstock*

Above left: Soybeans are delicious either dried or cooked as edamame while still green. Photo courtesy fotokostic/ Thinkstock. Above right: Saving seeds for soybean plants is easy: just avoid the temptation of eating the whole harvest! Photo courtesy Francois Lariviere/Thinkstock

Soybeans are great self-advertisers. The plants radiate a clean solidity, robustness and lushness that culminate in the satisfaction of eating the mild and nutty cooked beans. They are a sustainable and totally appropriate food plant for our current and future sustenance. Try them—you'll love them!

NITROGEN BOOSTER IN THE GARDEN

Like other legumes, soybeans have roots hosting nodule-forming bacteria that convert the nitrogen in air into a form that the plant can use. If soybeans have not been grown on your soil before, it is a good idea to inoculate the seed with the proper strain of nitrogen-fixing bacteria, which is available at farm and garden stores or through seed catalogues. Once you've had soybeans growing, the bacteria stay in the soil and help to improve future crops. I never fail to marvel at the increased production when I plant soybeans in an area in which they've been grown before.

Varieties. The few soybeans available in most seed catalogues are specifically edamame varieties, intended to be cooked in their green pods for four to five minutes. The soybeans offered by Salt Spring Seeds, however, are wonderful both as edamame beans and as dried beans with a full, rich flavour.

Agate, a New Mexico heirloom soybean, offers high yields, great eating quality and an early harvest; it is sometimes dry by mid-August.

Black Jet also matures early and is a good yielder of a thin-skinned, rich-tasting crop.

Champion, a yellow variety, is a good producer.

Gaia is the prettiest soybean you'll ever see. From Owen Bridge of Annapolis Seeds,[96] it's a cross between a green edamame and a black soybean.

Grand Forks is sweet, buttery and highly digestible.

Manitoba Brown tastes like a regular baking bean—and is also my favourite edamame pick!

Soil and Sun. While soybeans like a loose, well-drained loam best, they do well in a wide range of soil conditions. They prefer soil on the acidic side (pH from 5.8 to 7.0) and are not heavy feeders. Good news for gardeners is that soybeans are nitrogen-fixing plants that enrich the soil. Plant them where they will receive at least eight hours of sun a day.

Planting Time. Soybeans are a warm-weather crop, usually planted around the same time as corn. Soil and air temperatures of at least 55 to 60F (13 to 16C) are needed for good germination. The last week in May or the first week in June is the usual time to plant soybeans in southern Canada and the northern US.

Sowing. I plant my seeds about 1 inch (2.5 cm) deep, in rows 12 to 24 inches (30 to 61 cm) apart. Seeds need to absorb enough water to germinate, so if soil is sandy or low in moisture, plant them twice as deep. Soybeans do well either in raised beds or in traditional rows. I space my soybeans 6 inches (15 cm) apart, so that there is enough distance to safely hoe between them; they do well even at 3 inches (7.5 cm) apart. If you use a rototiller, it is most efficient to plant rows spaced slightly wider than the rototiller's breadth.

Maintenance. It is important to weed in the first weeks, as soybeans can be much slower to grow than the common weeds that love June weather. I usually hoe and hand-weed two or three times before the soybean plants form a canopy that shades out competition.

Reaching deep into the ground, soybeans have a fairly pronounced taproot that makes them quite tolerant of drought. The

most important time to ensure adequate soil moisture is from the plant's flowering in early summer through pod formation shortly afterwards. The drought tolerance of soybeans is a tremendous asset, as it is very evident that water will become a most precious resource in the coming decades.

I've been growing soybeans for about thirty years and haven't had any problems with pests or diseases.

Harvesting. Soybeans are ready to harvest as dry beans when the leaves have fallen and beans rattle in their pods, usually around mid-September on the West Coast or early September where summers are hot.

Pods can be picked individually or quickly stripped from the stalk with an upward motion of one hand. Wear gloves and hold the stalk lower down with the other hand. I usually gather my harvest in large buckets.

Threshing. Pods can be shelled one by one or can be rubbed apart by foot in a threshing box. To thresh by foot, the seeds must be dry enough so that a fingernail can't make an indentation. Chaff can be removed with suitable screening or blown away with a fan or hair dryer. I use a small air compressor with a blow-nozzle attachment.

I leave my seeds on screens in the sunlight for an extra day or more, or indoors in an airy spot if the weather is damp, to ensure maximum drying.

Yields. Yields aren't as high as for other beans, but soybeans are a much more substantial food, being about 35 percent protein. A 100-foot (30-m) row will fill a gallon jar with about 8 pounds (3.6 kg) of soybeans. Intensive raised beds can yield over 4 pounds (1.8 kg) per 36 square feet (3.4 m²).

Saving Seed. Soybean varieties don't cross, so maintaining your own seed is easy: just don't eat all your harvest, and remember to keep the biggest and best for planting!

HOW TO ENJOY SOYBEANS

Whether eaten as edamame or long-simmered, soybeans are deeply satisfying and sustaining.

Edamame. Soybeans are delicious when eaten at the fresh-shell stage, harvested just as the pods begin to lose their bright green colour. Steam or boil the unshelled pods for five minutes, with or without a little salt (depending upon your preference), then rinse them under cold water. Squeeze the beans out of the inedible pods and reheat them briefly. They are a fresh-taste sensation in July and August, and freeze well in plastic bags for year-round pleasure!

Simmered. Homegrown soybeans need about 90 minutes of simmering after an overnight soak in order to be cooked al dente. Most commercial types will need at least 3 hours' cooking. Soybeans can replace other dried beans in many recipes, and are more filling than pintos or kidneys because they are higher in both protein and oil. For this reason, when substituting soybeans for other legumes you can reduce the required amount by a third.

CHAPTER 10

Wheat

Wheat (*Triticum* spp.) is yet another nourishing, grow-your-own food that, to my mind, is awaiting our fuller embrace. While it has been a major crop for North America—in fact, the Canadian prairies were considered the breadbasket of the world for many decades—it was grown primarily to be processed into flour.[97]

RETHINKING WHOLE WHEAT

This book is about the great crops that we could be welcoming into our lives and growing as whole food. I've been convinced since my early days as a farmer that there are lots of good reasons to prepare wheat whole in the same manner as rice.

Wheat is falling out of favour these days because so many people have an intolerance to its gluten. "Gluten-free" claims are now used to promote many foods; I have done the same in some of these chapters. However, I don't think it fair to blame wheat itself for creating unpleasant allergic reactions. Before eliminating wheat from your diet, consider the following points.

First, many more people seem to be gluten intolerant today than just a few decades ago. How did so many people so quickly develop such a sensitivity?

Opposite: This wheat hails from Tibet. *Karen Mouat photo*

Secondly, I've had many people tell me that, despite experiencing gluten intolerance in North America, they had no trouble eating bread and pastries when travelling in Europe. How does one make sense of that?

I believe there is an obvious answer—and it points to the same glyphosate herbicide that I discuss in my chapter about soybeans. While wheat is not a GMO crop that has been genetically modified to survive applications of Roundup as soybeans are, it nevertheless is sometimes sprayed with Roundup, by planes at harvest time. This aerial spraying of herbicide, designed to destroy all other vegetation and to make combining easier and more efficient, has taken place in North America only in the past few decades and is not done in Europe.

So could it be that, instead of gluten intolerance, many North Americans actually are struggling with glyphosate intolerance? That it's the residue of this herbicide in our breads, breakfast cereals and crackers that is affecting our digestive tracts? From what I see and hear, people who eat wheat that is organically grown and unsprayed have far fewer digestive issues than those who ingest conventionally grown wheat.

In a recent book entitled *Grain of Truth: Why Eating Wheat Can Improve Your Health,*[98] author Stephen Yafa has an alternative explanation for gluten intolerance. He states that, at most, only 6 of us out of 100 have any real difficulty in digesting the gluten found in wheat, rye and barley. Rather, it is the way grain is milled and processed by large industrial manufacturers and bakers that is the problem. Whole grains are easily digested by most people if naturally fermented over two days, rather than the four hours allotted for this process in commercial bakeries. He cites a Harvard study of 117,500 men and women over a 25-year period that revealed that people who eat a whole, grain-rich diet lower their risk of cardiovascular disease by 20 percent and increase their lifespan by at least 6 percent.

Similarly, a 2015 study by the Harvard T.H. Chan School of Public Health claimed that eating more whole grains reduces overall mortality rates by up to 15 percent.[99] This finding was reinforced in their 2016 study, which claimed that those who ate 2½ ounces (70 grams) per day of whole grains had a 22 percent lower risk of total mortality when compared to those who ate few or no whole grains.[100]

THE WHOLE STORY ABOUT EATING WHEAT

When we grow ancient wheat organically in our own gardens, we restore it to the original role it had in nourishing us: as a healthy whole food to be eaten in the simplest of ways.

Unrefined, wheat is loaded with the B vitamins thiamine, riboflavin, niacin, pantothenic acid, B_6 and folate. It is rich in the minerals manganese and selenium, and also contains iron, magnesium, phosphorus, zinc and copper. It is very high in fibre and extremely low in saturated fat, cholesterol and sodium.[101]

The wheat germ—the embryo of the kernel—is a valuable source of vitamin E, which supports the immune system and is recommended as a cancer preventative. To benefit from this, though, it is essential to eat wheat as the whole food it is. In most of the refined versions on grocery store shelves, more than half of wheat's nutrients are lost. By choosing to eat organic whole wheat, you will be getting all the goodness of the bran, the germ and the endosperm.

At about 13 percent, wheat is relatively high in protein as compared to other grains. In fact, wheat contributes more calories and proteins to the world's diet than any other cereal crop. It contains phytochemicals including lignans, phenolic acids, phytic acid, plant sterols and saponins, and is a good source of antioxidants.[102]

When embraced as the important whole food it can be, wheat is considered an anti-cancer food,[103] reduces inflammation; lowers the risk of gallstones; heart disease and diabetes; and can contribute to a longer and healthier life.[104]

A WONDER WHEAT FROM ETHIOPIA

When I was in Ethiopia in 1993, I learned that the diversity of wheat varieties grown there was immense. Like their barleys, Ethiopians grew and knew their wheats, and maintained records on thousands of cultivars.

Out of all those choices, an Ethiopian farmer gave me a few heads of one variety that he especially liked. As I multiplied it for a few seasons, I became extremely impressed with the results. Compared to all the other wheat varieties I had been trialling for six to ten years, this one was much faster in reaching maturity. In fact, I harvested it a few times after only ninety days, about two weeks earlier than any other wheat I was growing.

I knew that a lot of the wheat-breeding work in Canada for many decades consisted of getting cultivars to mature earlier; sometimes even a day or two was considered an important improvement. I was shaking my head in disbelief and wonderment that I had a wheat variety ready for harvest so much earlier than the standard Canadian wheats.

I knew that my Ethiopian wheat was not a bread wheat; my farmer friend explained that it was best cooked as a whole grain. Still, if it grew to maturity as quickly as my barleys do in cool coastal British Columbia, surely there were other wheats—possibly bread wheats—that might mature even earlier.

That got me thinking about how cultural priorities and the way we eat foods so strongly determine the nature of the crops we choose. I reminded myself of how the amaranths that were grown for seed in Central and South America were so different from the amaranths grown for greens in Southeast Asia.

I named my special wheat "Blue Tinge Ethiopian," as there was a blue hue to both the dark seed heads and the brown seeds. When I cooked this wheat by simmering the kernels for an hour, I found it to be nutty, sweet and substantial eaten on its own. This left me wondering why I had never heard of wheat being simply cooked as a whole grain.

After a few years of multiplying my crop, I sent some of it to Monica Spiller of The Whole Grain Connection in California.[105] After a few years, it was being successfully and enthusiastically grown on hundreds of acres by members of her grain co-op. She informed me that my Blue Tinge Ethiopian was an emmer wheat. That was quite interesting to me, because all the other emmers I was growing had difficult-to-remove hulls. Emmer wheat has a plump grain that is longer than regular wheat grain. It is a hard wheat, well suited to making pasta and very popular in Italy, where it is called *farro*. It is lower in gluten than other wheat, but higher in protein and fibre.

GROWING AND KNOWING ORGANIC WHEAT

I'm still growing and selling Blue Tinge Ethiopian emmer and still wondering if, one day, more Canadians will be enjoying and appreciating similar organic wheats in whole-food form.

Varieties. In addition to Blue Tinge Ethiopian emmer, I've grown many other kinds of wheats during my farming career. I still maintain about a dozen. They are quite different from each other, and come from Egypt, Alaska, Mexico, Tibet, Spain, Canada and the Middle East. All have good flavour and texture when cooked as a whole grain.

One of my wheats is Red Fife, often called the "grandma" of Canadian wheats; it was the first to be grown in this country, and remained the prime wheat grown until 1900. Yet it had almost disappeared until a friend of mine, Sharon Rempel, grew a pound (0.45 kg) of it in 1988,[106] then kept multiplying and promoting it. Since then—because it makes such unforgettable artisan bread

Above left: Red Fife is often called the "grand-ma" of Canadian wheats. *Above right:* Varieties of emmer wheat generally have large heads and large seeds. *Both photos by Karen Mouat*

The characteristic look of wheat in a field. *Karen Mouat photo*

with a reddish-golden crust—Red Fife has had a phenomenal resurgence in popularity.

Another Canadian wheat that I maintain is Marquis. It was the top wheat of the Canadian Prairies for many decades, but it has now been largely forgotten. This is a shame, as it is a reliable wheat well documented for its superior baking quality, good flavour, high yields and disease resistance.[107]

I've also been growing an ancient wheat called Kamut since 1988. It has a very large seed and tastes more like corn than wheat. When a cereal conglomerate managed to patent the name "Kamut" in the '90s,[108] I began calling it "Khorasan" wheat instead, because it originated in the Khorasan region of modern-day Iran.

First cultivated during the Neolithic Age and early Bronze Age, einkorn wheat dates back ten thousand years and is still grown in the Basque country of northern Spain/southern France. Eaten whole or ground in baking, it has superb flavour but is low-yielding because of its small kernels.

The Tibetan wheat I have is traditionally roasted, finely milled, then mixed with ghee, salt and black tea, and made into dumplings. I've cooked this myself and I like its musky flavour.

My amber-coloured Brazilian wheat comes from Lavras. It is always my best producer in all conditions, growing up to 6 feet (180 cm) and being reliably disease-free.

White Sonora wheat is one of the oldest surviving North American wheats, brought to the southwest US by Spanish missionaries in 1691. Mostly awnless, and compact in the garden, it is a very soft white wheat that is excellent for making tortillas.

Utrecht Blue wheat comes from Holland and is one of my favourites because of its large, striking silvery-blue heads.

So far, I haven't found out much about how wheat varieties planted in the fall fare in other parts of Canada, except to hear that a cultivar called Soissons is especially winter hardy. Generally, growing wheat is about the same as growing barley, although the former is not as cold hardy and takes a little longer to mature.

Above left: Black Einkorn is a very ancient crop, dating back ten thousand years. *Above right:* Utrecht Blue wheat is very ornamental. *Both photos by Dan Jason*

Soil and Sun. Grains tend to "lodge" or fall over in very fertile earth, so it's better to plant them in your less enriched areas. Choose areas that receive at least seven hours of sun a day.

Planting Time. In general, wheat can be planted as early as the ground can be worked in spring.

It can be fall-planted as well, with the winter-hardy cultivar Soissons being especially good for colder climates.

In coastal British Columbia (zones 7 to 9), September, October or November sowings produce dependable results with most hardy wheats. Last winter was especially long, cold and snowy, and all my wheat cultivars survived well in my Salt Spring Island garden, following a mid-September sowing.

Sowing. To first-time growers, I recommend sowing grains 1 inch (2.5 cm) or so apart, in rows. After a season of multiplying them, planting in blocks works well. Cover the seeds lightly, but try to conceal them all so that birds don't discover them.

Maintenance. Very little maintenance is required, except to pull out noxious weeds like thistle and bindweed in the early stages. As grains grow, they quickly shade out almost everything else.

Harvesting. Both late-fall and early-spring plantings are harvested in late July or early August, allowing for midsummer sowings of other crops. Harvest the ripe seed when the plants have dried down completely in the garden, by picking or cutting the individual heads.

Threshing. Thresh by hand or foot rubbing. I use my simple wooden threshing box; shuffling my feet over the hard grains removes the chaff from the kernels. I follow by quickly cleaning the seed with the nozzle attachment on my air compressor. Fanning, screening and winnowing work too.

Yields. It's easy to grow a few pounds of wheat in your own garden. A patch 10 by 15 feet (3 by 4.6 m) can yield 15 pounds (6.8 kg).

Saving Seed. As with the other grains in this book, saving seed simply means not eating your entire crop.

HOW TO ENJOY ANCIENT WHEAT

Few people realize that wheat grains can be cooked whole. They provide much more nutritional benefit than the consumption of bread or pasta.

Berry Nourishing Meal Ideas. Homegrown wheat berries will cook up, at a low simmer, in about an hour. Once cooked, here are a few simple, easy ways to enjoy them.

1. Add wheat berries to soups, to make the broth considerably more substantial.

2. Wheat berries make a nice addition to cooked rice, in the proportion of 1:3.

3. Wheat berries work well in combination with black beans, particularly when seasoned with garlic, ginger and cumin.

4. They complement red beans too, especially with hot sauce.

5. Try wheat berries in a simple tomato salad for 2: Add 1 cup (250 mL) chopped tomatoes and ¼ cup (60 mL) chopped mild onion to 1 cup (250 mL) cooked and cooled wheat berries. Season with a simple oil and vinegar dressing and dash of salt and pepper.

6. Add peas to please: Just before 1 cup (250 mL) of wheat berries have finished cooking, add ½ cup (120 mL) fresh or frozen peas and 1 tablespoon (15 mL) finely chopped garlic greens or chives. Add 2 teaspoons (10 mL) butter or oil, then salt to taste and simmer 5 to 10 more minutes. Results are fast and filling.

7. Sprouted wheat berries can be used to make exciting salads. Here's an easy combination for 4: To 2 cups (475 mL) of sprouted wheat berries, add a diced cucumber, diced sweet pepper, diced tomato, diced small celery stalk, chopped scallion and handful of chopped parsley. Toss with 1 cup (250 mL) oil/lemon dressing, cover and refrigerate overnight before serving.

8. Easy and cheesy casserole for 4: Steam 3 cups cubed squash with 1 cup (250 mL) diced carrots for 15 minutes. In a large casserole, toss the cooked squash and carrots with 2 cups (475 mL) cooked wheat berries and 2 tablespoons (30 mL) chopped chives. Sprinkle with 2 cups (475 mL) shredded cheddar cheese and broil for 5 minutes or until cheese is melted and lightly browned.

 ## Other Grains to Grow and Eat

Rye, oats and triticale are other healthy grains that can be grown just like wheat, and cooked up as whole seeds by simmering them for about an hour.

COLD-RESISTANT RYE

While most people in North America are familiar with rye (*Secale cereale*) in bread and crackers, few think of growing it to eat as a whole grain. This is commonly done in Scandinavian countries, as rye has a loose-fitting hull that is very easily threshed. Those who eat it enjoy the benefits of its generous portions of fibre, manganese, phosphorus, copper, pantothenic acid and magnesium.[109] Note that rye contains gluten.

In the garden, rye is very cold hardy and often is planted as a winter cover crop and a soil conditioner. Its deep roots bring up minerals from the subsoil and are excellent for breaking up heavy clay soils.

HULLESS OATS

Oats such as the classic Canadian heirloom Rodney (*Avena sativa*) present another way of cooking up goodness from the garden when they are honoured as the whole grains they are. Oats are a powerhouse source of manganese and molybdenum, along with

phosphorus, copper, biotin, thiamine, magnesium, chromium, zinc, protein and fibre.[110]

Oats don't tolerate cold weather as well as barley or rye, and are best sown at around the same time as wheat. It is more fun to harvest oats than other grains, as the kernels can easily be stripped off the stalk with an upward swipe of the hand. For home-garden growing, there are a few varieties with "naked" hulls that can be easily threshed, such as Streaker hulless oats (*Avena nuda*).

ROBUST TRITICALE

Triticale (*X Triticosecale Wittmack*) is a robust cross between wheat and rye, with a pleasant, mild, nutty flavour. It is a good source of phosphorus and manganese, in addition to magnesium, zinc, copper, iron, thiamine, riboflavin, niacin, vitamin B_6, folate and pantothenic acid.[111]

Simple to grow and thresh, it is almost as hardy and vigorous as rye, with the advantage of a less massive root system that makes it easier to remove after harvest.

This grain interests me because it is the only new grain I know and grow that has been created by modern agriculture. All the other grains in this book have existed in similar forms for thousands of years.

Above left: Unlike wheats and barleys, oats have their seed heads hanging down. *Above middle:* Rodney is a famous Canadian heirloom variety of oats. *Above right:* The seeds of Streaker oats separate cleanly and easily from their hulls. *All photos by Karen Mouat*

CHAPTER 11

Soaking and Sprouting
GRAINS AND SEEDS

By sprouting your own homegrown grains and seeds, or an organic supply from a local source, you can enjoy fresh-tasting, healthy sprouts for salads, wraps, sandwiches or stir-fries. Or add these whole foods to raw granola, hummus, soups and smoothies. Sprouted grains and seeds are best eaten as fresh as possible, so keep an ongoing supply.

AWAKEN THE ENERGY IN GRAINS AND SEEDS

Sprout grains or seeds—or simply give them a good soak—to awaken their life-giving energies and to provide yet another way to savour their delicious nourishment!

- **Amaranth Seeds:** Tiny, super-nourishing, red-tinged sprouts are ready in 2–4 days and can be added to just about anything.

- **Barley:** Grains sprout quickly, in 1–3 days, and are sweet and satisfying.

- **Buckwheat Groats:** Unroasted groats (the seeds with the hulls removed) are best for sprouting buckwheat, and are ready in 1–3 days.

- **Flaxseed:** Because flaxseed can be mucilaginous (which means that, as with chia seeds, a gel sac forms around each seed when exposed to water), it may not grow noticeable roots. Don't worry about this. Simply soaking up water will bring the seed out of dormancy and boost the

Opposite: Sprouting is an easy and tasty way to enjoy whole seeds and grains.

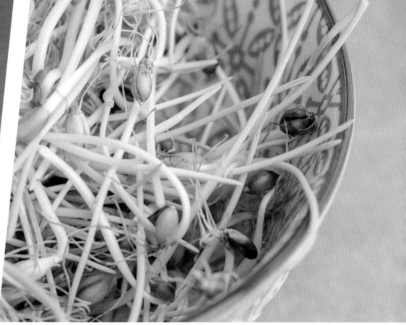

Above left: Rye seeds only take two to three days to sprout. *Above right:* Sprouts are best eaten as soon as possible, so keep a supply going all the time!

available nutrients. What's more, soaking may eliminate phytic acid and increase mineral absorption.

- Instead of using a sprouter, soak flaxseed in a shallow dish or tray, adding twice as much water as seed, and stirring it. Your flaxseed will be ready to eat 4–12 hours later, having absorbed its fill of water.

- **Oats:** Hulless oats are best for tender, mildly sweet sprouts that are ready in 1–3 days.

- **Quinoa:** Sprouts grow quickly, and can usually be eaten within 24 hours. Because quinoa contains saponins, your rinse water may appear slightly sudsy; rinse the seeds extremely well to remove this foaminess. If you are sensitive to saponins, you may want to limit your consumption of quinoa sprouts. But once well rinsed, they are usually well tolerated and are lovely to eat, as they have a nutty, mildly beet-like flavour.

- **Rye:** These sweet and nutritious sprouts are ready in 2–3 days.

- **Soybeans:** You may wish to cover your soybeans with a dark cloth to blanch the sprouts; this will keep them more tender. Do not eat sprouted soybeans raw; they are more digestible when steamed lightly in stir-fries or added to Asian-inspired soups. Sprouts are ready in 2–6 days.

- **Styrian Hulless Pumpkin Seeds:** Sprout for 1 day, or eat after a good soak. A soak works well for large seeds. Leave them in a bowl for 1–4 hours with twice as much water, allowing the seed to develop a bulge; this signals the end of dormancy. Despite a lack of roots, soaked seeds are alive, making them extra nutritious. Soaking also eliminates enzyme inhibitors.

- **Triticale:** Tasty, sweet sprouts are ready for harvest in 2–3 days.
- **Wheat:** Sweet-tasting sprouts appear in 2–3 days.[112]

You'll find several types of sprouters online or at your local health food store. Or simply use a large Mason jar with a metal or plastic screen lid, or with cheesecloth secured over the top with an elastic band.

Good rinsing and drainage are essential. Give your sprouts a thorough rinse two to three times daily, and follow this with a good shake to get as much water off them and out of the sprouter as possible.

10 STEPS TO SPROUTS

1. Check your grain or seeds to ensure that they are free of any debris and imperfect grains or seeds. Anything that has been compromised will not sprout and could rot in the sprouting process.
2. Soak in cool water, to wake up your dormant dry grains or seeds and to set off the sprouting process. Cover the grain or seed with at least 3 times as much water. (It doesn't hurt to add extra water.) Stir the water to ensure all the grain or seeds have even contact with it, and leave them to soak for up to 12 hours.
3. Skim off any debris or grain or seeds floating on the water. "Floaters" often indicate a dead seed.
4. By the end of the soaking, the grain or seeds should be swollen and have doubled or tripled in size; if not, allow more soaking time.
5. Place your well-soaked grain or seeds into a sterile sprouter or Mason jar with a screen lid or a cheesecloth secured over the top with an elastic band.
6. Rinsing is critical in growing healthy sprouts. Use lots of cool water to give the sprouts a thorough high-pressure rinse over the sink. (So that this nutritious water doesn't go to waste, you can catch it in a container to dump into your garden.) Rinse 2–4 times daily.

7. Drain as much of the water from your sprouts as possible; shake them upside down and be diligent about not leaving moisture to pool in your sprouter. Insufficient draining can lead to mould; this is the most common reason for failure when growing sprouts.

8. Store your sprouter on an airy counter or any place with good circulation and out of direct sunlight. If the weather is hot and humid, positioning it near a fan works well.

9. When your sprouts are ready to eat—usually after 1–6 days, depending upon what you are sprouting and how you prefer to eat them—give them a final, thorough rinse with cool water. Then shake them vigorously before leaving them in the open air for a few more hours, to dry further before storing them in the refrigerator. The drier they are, the better they will keep. Whizzing them in a salad spinner or swinging them around in an absorbent cloth bag or tea towel are good ways to shake the water off those sprouts.

10. Once they are as dry as you can get them, store your sprouts in a sealed container or a produce bag in the refrigerator. If you are concerned that the sprouts are still too damp, tuck in some paper towelling or a clean cloth to sponge up moisture, or punch a few air-holes into a plastic bag and use that for storage. Kept cold, your sprouts should last several days. However, they are best eaten as soon as possible, so keep them coming and eat lots every day!

USE GRAINS TO GROW GRASS FOR JUICING

Consider growing some grass with your grain seed. Made into a juice (using an extracting juicer), grass is a powerful source of nutrients and, because of its high content of chlorophyll, a powerful detoxifier.[113]

It is so powerful, in fact, that you are advised to drink it sparingly; a maximum of two 1-ounce (30-mL) shots per day or every other day is recommended, preferably on an empty stomach and a half-hour before eating.[114] You can also add other fruits and vegetables to your juicer, to dilute the effect and to boost flavour. Wheatgrass or grass from other grains should not be consumed for long periods of time, but rather sporadically to purify the body.[115]

Even if the grain used contains gluten in its seed form, juice made from its young grass will be gluten-free.[116]

The trick to growing healthful and vigorous grasses for juicing is to give them lots of water—but not so much that they rot. Do not eat wheatgrass if it is showing signs of mould, even at the root level. Dispose of it, re-sterilize your equipment and grow a fresh batch.

Grasses do best at room temperature: too hot and they dry out; too cold and they will not grow. To prevent mould and mildew, place your growing trays inside where there is good air circulation but no direct sunlight.

All the grains in this book can be grown into grasses for juicing:

- Barley
- Oats
- Rye
- Triticale
- Wheat

Above: All you need is a Mason jar with a piece of cheesecloth to create a rainbow of sprouts.

STEP-BY-STEP DIRECTIONS FOR GROWING GRASS

1. Start off by soaking your grain seeds, following steps 1–5 in 10 Steps to Sprouts, on pages 91–92.

2. Once your sprouted grains are all sporting a very short "tail," tip them into a clean planting tray containing a layer of organic potting soil and peat moss (mixed 3:1), coconut coir or another growing medium. There are many options available; a quick Web search will let you explore the alternatives. Spread the sprouts gently so that they connect with the growing medium and are not piled on top of each other; they must be able to root into the soil or coir. Do not crowd your seed, as this encourages mould.

3. Water the seed well, but don't create a swamp! The grain needs to be moist but not submerged.

4. Cover with another tray or a piece of dark plastic, to keep the grain moist and to encourage root growth.

5. Water each morning for the next 3 days.

6. On day 4 or 5 after planting—once the grass starts pushing up your top tray or plastic—uncover it. It will need enough light to turn green; in winter, this may require grow lights.

7. Keep the grass watered; don't let the tray dry out and become light in weight.

8. When the grass blades begin to fork into two, this is the signal that it is at its sweetest and most nutritious and is ready to eat! Use clean scissors to harvest your crop. Harvest straight from the tray for optimal freshness, and toss a handful into an extracting juicer for a healthful shot of goodness. Store wheatgrass in the fridge in an airtight container for up to a week. Tuck in some paper towelling or a clean cloth to sponge up excess moisture.

GROW BUCKWHEAT "LETTUCE" MICROGREENS

Grow buckwheat microgreens—called buckwheat "lettuce"—from unhulled buckwheat seed from your own garden, using a method similar to growing grass from grains.

Follow the Step-by-step Directions for Growing Grass on pages 94–95, except for steps 4 and 6; microgreens do not need to be covered at any stage of their growth.

Rinsing vigorously everyday will help to remove the hulls and to keep your crop moist. After 10 days of growing, most of the hulls should have fallen away. Snip away at these rutin-rich greens to make salads, sandwiches and stir-fries!

How to Grind Flour

Using freshly ground flour to make your bread produces delicious results and superior nutrition compared to bread made with store-bought flours. And it can be done with nothing but a coffee grinder! If you haven't grown your own, organic whole grain berries can usually be purchased cheaply at your health food store or supermarket.

For an even grind, don't fill your grinder more than halfway. The longer you grind, the finer your flour will be. It takes about a minute to grind your flour completely. If you want your flour even finer, you can sift it through a fine mesh sifter and then regrind the larger parts that don't pass through.

After experiencing the flavour of bread made with freshly ground flour, you're likely to consider the purchase of a regular grain mill to be well worth it!

Recipes

Whole Grain Granola

MAKES ABOUT 8 CUPS (2 L).

Granola is not only crunchy and delicious, it's very forgiving—it will take just about any combination of oats, grain flakes, nuts, seeds and dried fruits you like. This recipe gives small-plot farmers the option to add in whatever they've got growing this season. *Vegan* IF YOU USE MAPLE OR BIRCH SYRUP

4 cups (950 mL) rolled oats
1 cup (250 mL) raw pumpkin seeds
1 cup (250 mL) raw cashews
1 cup (250 mL) raw hazelnuts
1 cup (250 mL) raw almonds
¾ cup (180 mL) quinoa flakes
¾ cup (180 mL) raw sesame seeds
¾ cup (180 mL) raw sunflower seeds
½ cup (120 mL) raw flaxseeds

⅔ cup (160 mL) coconut oil
⅓ cup (80 mL) honey, maple syrup or birch syrup
1 tsp (5 mL) kosher salt
⅔ cup (160 mL) unsweetened large flake coconut
1 cup (250 mL) any combination of dried raisins, dates, currants or apricots

1. Preheat oven to 300F (150C).

2. Mix oats, nuts, quinoa and seeds in a large bowl. Melt coconut oil and honey or syrup in a small pot set over medium heat. Stir in salt. Pour over the dry ingredients and mix thoroughly.

3. Spread granola into two 9 × 13-inch (22.5 × 32-cm) baking dishes. Bake for 45 minutes, stirring every 10 minutes and switching position of pans halfway through. Add coconut and dried fruit for the final 5 minutes.

4. Cool on a rack to room temperature. Store in an airtight container in a cool, dark place, or if granola consumption is not as rapid in your household, freeze half the yield. Granola will keep for up to 4 weeks at room temperature, and 6 months in the freezer.

Continued on page 100

Whole Grain Breakfast Bowl

It's a good idea to keep a batch of cooked whole grain always ready in the fridge, to add to salads or soup or for a quick breakfast bowl. Warm up servings of cooked whole grain on the stove with a little water, milk or nut milk. Then start adding toppings—flax, sunflower or pumpkin seeds, yogurt, berries, fresh fruit, granola. So easy, such a good start to the day.

Savoury Breakfast Scones

MAKES 12 SCONES.

These scones are great with melting butter and honey for a quick breakfast, or an excellent accompaniment for a soup and salad dinner.

2 cups (475 mL) whole spelt flour

2 tsp (10 mL) baking powder

½ tsp (2.5 mL) baking soda

¼ tsp (1 mL) salt

2 tsp (10 mL) dried rosemary

6 Tbsp (90 mL) cold butter, diced

½–¾ cup (125-180 mL) yogurt

2 tsp (10 mL) Dijon mustard

½ cup (120 mL) chopped green onion

1 cup + 2 Tbsp (250 + 30 mL) grated sharp cheddar cheese, divided

1. Preheat oven to 400F (205C) and line 2 baking sheets with parchment.

2. Combine dry ingredients in the bowl of a food processor. Pulse briefly to mix, then add butter and pulse until butter is broken into pea-sized pieces.

3. In a medium bowl, whisk together ½ cup (120 mL) of the yogurt and the mustard. Stir in flour and butter mixture, adding additional yogurt only if the mixture is too crumbly to cohere. (Flours differ in their ability to absorb liquid.) Stir in onions and 1 cup (250 mL) cheddar cheese, reserving 2 tablespoons (30 mL) cheddar for topping the scones.

4. Tip dough onto a lightly floured surface and pat into a circle about ½-inch (1.25-cm) thick. Divide into 12 equal wedges and place on baking sheets.

5. Bake for 8 minutes. Sprinkle reserved cheese overtop, return scones to the oven and bake until tops are golden brown and cheese is bubbly, about 7 minutes. Remove from the oven and serve right away. Store any leftovers in a tin and eat within two days. (On the second day they're great toasted.)

Whole Wheat, Amaranth and Blueberry Muffins

MAKES 12 MUFFINS.

There's something magic about amaranth and blueberries—perhaps it's the colour, perhaps the complementary flavours of earth and fruit. For this recipe, cook dried amaranth and water at a ratio of 1:1. *Vegan* IF YOU USE FLAX EGGS

2 cups (475 mL) Red Fife or other whole wheat flour

1 Tbsp (15 mL) baking powder

2 tsp (10 mL) ground cardamom

¼ tsp (1 mL) salt

2 large eggs (or substitute 2 vegan flax eggs; see sidebar below)

½ cup (120 mL) organic cane sugar

1 tsp (5 mL) vanilla

¼ cup (60 mL) melted coconut oil, at room temperature

½ cup (120 mL) cooked amaranth (for cooking instructions, see How to Enjoy Amaranth Seed, page 22)

1 cup (250 mL) wild blueberries

½ cup (120 mL) chopped pecans

1. Preheat oven to 375F (180C) and lightly oil a standard 12-cup muffin tin, or line with parchment liners.

2. In a medium bowl, whisk dry ingredients together. In a separate bowl, beat eggs until frothy and light in colour. Whisk in sugar, followed by remaining wet ingredients and amaranth, whisking vigorously to break up any clumps of grain.

3. Stir wet ingredients into dry just until mixed, then fold in blueberries and pecans. Spoon into muffin tin. Bake for 25 minutes, or until tops are lightly browned.

4. Cool in the muffin tin on a rack for 10 minutes, then remove muffins by carefully running a knife around each one. Eat warm or at room temperature. Store in a covered tin in a cool place for up to 4 days. These muffins freeze well.

Flax Eggs

Flaxseed eggs are a good vegan substitute for chicken eggs. For each flax egg, whisk 1 Tbsp (15 mL) milled flaxseeds with 2½ Tbsp (37 mL) water. Allow to stand for 5 minutes before using.

Whole Grain Blueberry Cinnamon Rolls

MAKES 12 ROLLS.

Who doesn't love cinnamon rolls for breakfast, at elevenses or during a break on a long paddling trip? Overnight option: make the dough and shape the buns the night before, refrigerate until morning and allow to warm up for about an hour before baking.

DOUGH

1½ cups (350 mL) whole spelt flour

¼ tsp (1 mL) salt

¼ cup (60 mL) milled flaxseeds

1½ cups (350 mL) + ⅓ cup (80 mL) whole wheat pastry flour, divided

2 Tbsp (30 mL) butter

½ cup (120 mL) maple syrup

1 cup (250 mL) milk

2¼ tsp (10.1 mL) dry active yeast

1 egg, beaten

FILLING

¼ cup (60 mL) melted butter

¾ cup (180 mL) packed brown sugar

2 Tbsp (30 mL) cinnamon

½ tsp (2.5 mL) ground cardamom

1½ cups (350 mL) frozen blueberries

1 Tbsp (15 mL) whole spelt flour

TOPPING

1 Tbsp (15 mL) flaxseeds (optional)

1. In a medium bowl, whisk together spelt flour, salt, flaxseeds and 1½ cups (350 mL) of the pastry flour. Set aside.

2. Heat butter and maple syrup in a small saucepan over medium heat until butter is melted. Whisk in milk and heat until mixture is lukewarm. Remove from heat and sprinkle yeast over top. Once yeast has bloomed (after about 5 minutes), whisk egg into milk and yeast mixture.

3. Make a well in dry ingredients and pour in the milk mixture. Stir until well combined—the dough will be quite wet—and start mixing in remaining ⅓ cup (80 mL) whole wheat pastry flour, 1 tablespoon (30 mL) at a time, until dough is smooth enough to knead.

4. Tip onto a lightly floured work surface and with floured hands, knead briefly and form into a ball. Return dough to bowl, dust with flour, cover and allow to rise in a warm place until doubled in bulk, about 1 hour.

Continued on page 106

5. Meanwhile, in a small bowl mix together melted butter, brown sugar, cinnamon and cardamom.

6. Spread a large piece of parchment paper on work surface and sprinkle with flour. With floured hands or a rolling pin, pat or roll the dough into a rectangle of about 12 × 8 inches (30 × 20 cm).

7. Spread the dough with brown sugar and butter mixture, leaving a border of about ½ inch (1.25 cm). Toss frozen blueberries with flour and pat evenly onto dough. Starting with a long end, roll up the dough tightly, using parchment paper to help lift and shape it into an even log. Chill for 10 minutes, wrapped in the parchment paper.

8. Unwrap dough, and use a sharp knife to slice the dough into 12 even rolls. Place rolls on a parchment-lined baking sheet, cover with plastic and allow to proof for 30 minutes. At this point, you can also refrigerate the dough to bake the next morning, letting it come back to room temperature before baking.

9. While rolls are proofing, preheat oven to 350F (180C),

10. When rolls are ready, sprinkle tops with 1 tablespoon flaxseeds. Bake for 25 to 30 minutes, until puffy and golden brown. Remove from oven and cool in the pan on a rack for 10 minutes. Invert onto a piece of parchment paper.

11. Serve warm or cold, on their own or with a spoonful of cream cheese icing on top.

CREAM CHEESE ICING

MAKES ABOUT 1½ CUPS (350 ML).

¼ cup (60 mL) butter, softened

½ cup (120 mL) cream cheese, softened

1 cup (250 mL) sifted icing sugar

1 tsp (5 mL) lemon juice

1. Blend butter and cream cheese in a medium bowl. Beat in icing sugar until smooth, adding lemon juice at the end.

Morning Glory Quinoa Muffins

MAKES 18 MUFFINS.

The classic Morning Glory muffin with a seedy, grainy twist! *Vegan* IF YOU USE FLAX EGGS AND SOY YOGURT

2 cups (475 mL) chopped fresh or frozen rhubarb (or substitute applesauce or mashed banana)

1½ cups (350 mL) Red Fife or other whole wheat flour

¾ cup (180 mL) packed brown sugar

3 Tbsp (45 mL) milled flaxseeds

2 tsp (10 mL) baking soda

1 tsp (5 mL) cinnamon

¼ tsp (1 mL) ground cloves

¼ tsp (1 mL) salt

1 cup (250 mL) chopped dried apricots

½ cup (120 mL) dried currants

¾ cup (180 mL) chopped walnuts

1 large egg (or substitute 1 vegan flax egg; see sidebar on page 102)

1 cup (250 mL) plain yogurt (or substitute soy yogurt)

1 cup (250 mL) cooked quinoa (for cooking instructions, see How to Enjoy Quinoa Seed, page 64)

1. Preheat oven to 375F (180C) and lightly oil a standard 12-cup muffin tin and a 6-cup tin, or line with parchment liners.

2. Add rhubarb to a small saucepan with enough water to cover (about 1 cup/250 mL). Bring to a boil, then cover and reduce to a simmer. Cook for 10 minutes, until rhubarb is soft and has lost its shape. Strain liquid through a fine-meshed sieve into a bowl and use for other purposes (such as rhubarb syrup). Set aside cooked rhubarb.

3. Whisk dry ingredients in a medium bowl, then stir in dried fruits and nuts. In a separate bowl, whisk egg and yogurt, followed by rhubarb and cooked quinoa. Stir wet ingredients into dry just until mixed, making sure there are no clumps of flour at the bottom of the bowl.

4. Spoon into muffin tins and bake for 25 to 30 minutes, until tops are lightly browned and muffins pull away from the sides of the tin. (Note: These dense and moist muffins don't rise much over the top of the tin.)

5. Cool in the muffin tins on cooling racks for 10 minutes, then remove muffins by carefully running a knife around each one. Eat warm or at room temperature. Store in a covered tin in a cool place for up to 4 days. These muffins freeze well.

 To make rhubarb syrup from your leftover rhubarb juice, simply add sugar to taste and simmer for 5 minutes. Store in the fridge.

Sikil P'ak

MAKES ABOUT 2 CUPS (475 ML).

Raw pumpkin seeds shine in this favourite dip from the Yucatan Peninsula, with roots in Mayan culture. The smokiness of the charred vegetables is essential!

1½ cups (350 mL) hulled raw
    pumpkin seeds
1 Tbsp (15 mL) olive oil
2 plum tomatoes, cored and halved
1 jalapeno pepper, stemmed and
    halved (not seeded)
¼ white onion, separated
    into segments

2 cloves garlic, unpeeled
¼ cup (60 mL) chopped cilantro
¼ cup (60 mL) chopped chives
Juice of 1 lime
1 tsp (5 mL) kosher salt
1–2 Tbsp (15–30 mL) water (if needed)

1. Dry-roast pumpkin seeds in a large cast iron frying pan over medium heat for 5 to 7 minutes, or until they are lightly browned and have begun to pop. Pour into a bowl to cool.

2. Pour oil into the same frying pan and turn the heat up slightly. Place the tomatoes and jalapeno in the centre of the pan, cut side down. Scatter the onion around the periphery. Place the garlic at the edge where it will brown but not burn.

3. Turn garlic frequently and remove once it has browned on all sides. Cool to room temperature, peel and set aside. Blacken the edges of the tomatoes and jalapeno by leaving them cut side down for 5 minutes before turning. Press down on the onion segments to blacken them as well. Once vegetables are a good colour, after about 7 to 9 minutes, turn the heat down to medium low and soften them for about 3 minutes.

    (You can also do this whole step in the oven: coat the vegetables with olive oil and roast them at 400F/205C for about 20 minutes, or until browned and beginning to blacken, removing the garlic before it burns.)

4. Cool vegetables to room temperature. Combine seeds and vegetables in the bowl of a food processor and grind to a coarse paste.

5. Add cilantro, chives, lime juice and salt and pulse until combined. If the mixture is too stiff or crumbly, add water, 1 tablespoon (15 mL) at a time. (Note that this dip doesn't become a smooth purée like hummus—the graininess is part of its charm.) Taste and add more salt if needed.

6. Serve with tortilla chips, grilled vegetables or homemade crackers. Store covered in the fridge for up to a week.

Quinoa and Pumpkin Seed Fritters with Italian Salsa Verde and Labneh

MAKES ABOUT 35 FRITTERS, ABOUT 10 TO 12 SERVINGS.

Serve these crispy, highly flavoured fritters as an appetizer at cocktail hour. Or, for a casual weeknight dinner, stuff three into pita bread with some chopped arugula, chopped tomatoes and red onion, a dollop of labneh (page 112) and a spoonful of salsa verde (page 111). It doesn't get much better. There are a couple of tricks to frying the fritters—1) the oil should be between ¼ and ½-inch (0.6–1.25 cm) deep in the pan, and 2) the fritters need to "set" in the hot oil before flipping. If you try too soon, there's a danger they'll fall apart.

1 cup (250 mL) pumpkin seeds, divided

2 cups (475 mL) packed peppery greens (mustard or arugula)

2 cups (475 mL) cooked quinoa (for cooking instructions, see How to Enjoy Quinoa Seed, page 64)

½ cup (120 mL) chickpea flour

1 tsp (5 mL) kosher salt

1 tsp (5 mL) whole cumin seed, toasted

2 tsp (10 mL) fenugreek leaves

2 spring onions, white and green part, finely chopped

1 Tbsp (15 mL) minced garlic

1 tsp (5 mL) apple cider vinegar

2 eggs, beaten

½ cup (120 mL) coconut oil for frying

1. Dry-roast pumpkin seeds in a large cast iron frying pan over medium heat for 5 to 7 minutes, or until they are lightly browned and have begun to pop. Pour into a bowl to cool.

2. Coarsely grind ¾ cup (180 mL) of the toasted pumpkin seeds and leave the remainder whole. Finely chop the greens. In a medium bowl, combine all ingredients except eggs and coconut oil and mix thoroughly. Stir in the eggs with a fork, mixing thoroughly.

3. With damp hands, form small, flat patties using about 1½ tablespoons (22 mL) of the fritter mixture for each one. The mixture will be crumbly. Transfer finished patties to two parchment-lined baking sheets.

4. Preheat oven to 200F (95C) for keeping fritters warm.

5. Melt coconut oil in a cast iron frying pan over medium heat. Test oil for readiness by adding a few crumbs of fritter mixture—if it sizzles, the oil is ready.

6. Cook fritters in batches for 4 minutes on the first side, allowing the patties to set. Flip carefully and cook for 3 minutes on the second side. Drain on paper towels and keep warm in oven until all the fritters are done. (The later batches will cook more quickly than the first batches, so watch carefully, and add more coconut oil as necessary.)

7. You can also freeze any uncooked fritters on baking sheets, then transfer to resealable bags for storage. They will keep for up to three months.

ITALIAN SALSA VERDE

MAKES ABOUT ¾ CUP (180 ML).

Like harissa, this versatile and irresistible sauce has a thousand uses and as many variations. This one errs on the side of simplicity but the flavour is still just grand.

I packed cup (250 mL) cleaned and stemmed parsley

2 packed cups (475 mL) cleaned and stemmed cilantro

3 cloves garlic

2 Tbsp (30 mL) capers

I Tbsp (15 mL) caper brine

½ cup (120 mL) olive oil

Salt and pepper to taste

1. In the bowl of a food processor, combine all ingredients except olive oil and salt and pepper and pulse until coarsely ground. (You don't want as fine a texture as pesto.) Add the oil all at once and pulse a few more times until thoroughly combined. Taste for seasoning and add salt and pepper as needed.

2. Store in a covered container in the fridge and use on everything, from eggs to soup to vegetables to a plain bowl of cooked whole grains, and, of course, fritters. Will keep for up to 2 weeks.

Continued on page 112

HOMEMADE LABNEH

MAKES ABOUT 1¾ CUPS (415 ML).

For anyone interested in cheese-making at home, labneh is a
great way to start. It's simple and delicious, essentially a tangy
yogurt cream cheese, and ready in 24 hours.

2 cups (475 mL) plain dairy yogurt   ½ tsp (5 mL) salt

1. Whisk together yogurt and salt. Line a fine-meshed strainer with cheesecloth and set it over a bowl. Spoon the yogurt into the lined strainer,
   gather the ends of the cheesecloth together, twist and tie off with string
   or a twist-tie. Transfer to refrigerator and leave for 24 hours to allow the
   whey to drain and the yogurt to thicken. Transfer the finished labneh to
   a bowl with a cover and use within 5 days. Keep the whey and use it in
   pancakes, bread, muffins or other baked goods.

Edamame and Black Radish Pakoras with Fresh Tomato Chutney

MAKES ABOUT 25 PAKORAS, OR 6 TO 7 SERVINGS.

You can't always find black radishes, either in the garden or at the market. Daikon or red radishes of any variety will be just fine—it's that spicy radish heat we're after here. *Vegan* IF YOU USE COCONUT OIL

I cup (250 mL) cooked edamame beans (fresh or frozen; for cooking instructions, see How to Enjoy Soybeans, page 75)

1½ cups (350 mL) grated black radish (or substitute daikon radish)

¾ cup (180 mL) red onion, sliced into I-inch (2.5-cm) lengths

¼ cup (60 mL) grated carrot (about I small carrot)

I jalapeno pepper, finely chopped

2 Tbsp (30 mL) chopped cilantro

I Tbsp (15 mL) coconut oil, ghee or melted butter

¾ cup (180 mL) chickpea flour

I tsp (5 mL) ground coriander seeds

½ tsp (2.5 mL) asafoetida powder

I tsp (5 mL) mango powder (amchoor)

½ tsp (2.5 mL) salt

½ cup (120 mL) coconut oil, for frying

1. Combine vegetables, cilantro and 1 tablespoon (15 mL) coconut oil or ghee in a medium bowl.

2. Whisk dry ingredients together and stir into vegetable mixture until the vegetables are coated, making sure there's no flour remaining at the bottom of the bowl.

3. Preheat the oven to 200F (95C) for keeping pakoras warm.

4. Melt ½ cup (120 mL) coconut oil in a cast iron frying pan over medium heat. Test the temperature by dropping in a small piece of the pakora mixture—if it sizzles right away, the oil is ready.

Continued on page 114

5. For each pakora, gather a rough clump of about 1½ tablespoons (22 mL) of the mixture with your fingers. Place the first batch of pakoras in the oil, making sure not to crowd the pan. Cook for 2 to 3 minutes on one side to set the pakoras, then flip and cook another 2 to 3 minutes until browned and crisp.

6. Transfer cooked pakoras to a plate lined with paper towel and keep warm in the oven. Continue cooking in batches, adding more oil if necessary, until the mixture is finished.

7. Serve pakoras warm with Fresh Tomato Chutney.

FRESH TOMATO CHUTNEY

MAKES ABOUT 1½ CUPS (350 ML).

Make the chutney a couple of hours ahead to allow flavours to blend.

I tsp (5 mL) cumin seeds

2 medium tomatoes, roughly chopped

2 tsp (10 mL) chopped fresh ginger

2 tsp (10 mL) Sambal Oelek (or substitute I small jalapeno pepper, finely chopped)

I tsp (5 mL) lime juice

2 tsp (10 mL) sesame oil

¼ tsp (1 mL) salt

I Tbsp (15 mL) currants

2 Tbsp (30 mL) chopped cilantro

1. Toast cumin seeds in a cast iron frying pan over medium heat until seeds are aromatic and begin to pop, about 5 minutes. Cool seeds slightly and then coarsely grind in a mortar and pestle.

2. Place all ingredients in the bowl of a food processor and pulse several times until chutney is liquid but still somewhat chunky. Store in a covered container in the fridge. The chutney will keep for several days but is best eaten right away.

Emmer Dolmades with Avgolemono Sauce

MAKES 30 TO 45 DOLMADES.

The chewy texture of whole emmer adds a satisfying new dimension to this Middle Eastern/Mediterranean classic, which is usually made with rice.

1 cup (250 mL) raw emmer grains
2 cups (475 mL) water
1 cup (250 mL) raw sunflower seeds
2 tsp (10 mL) cumin seeds
½ cup (120 mL) packed chopped fresh mint
1 cup (250 mL) packed chopped fresh dill
½ cup (120 mL) chopped spring onions (about 4 onions)
1 Tbsp (15 mL) minced garlic (about 2 large cloves garlic)

½ cup (120 mL) dried currants
1 tsp (5 mL) salt
1 tsp (5 mL) pepper
3 Tbsp (45 mL) sunflower seed butter
2 Tbsp (30 mL) olive oil
2 Tbsp (30 mL) lemon juice
1 Tbsp (15 mL) grated lemon zest
16-oz (475-mL) jar grape leaves, drained
4–6 cups (1–1.4 L) vegetable stock, divided

1. Rinse emmer grains under running water. Combine emmer and water in a medium saucepan, cover, bring to the boil, reduce heat and simmer for 40 minutes. The texture should be chewy and nutty. Remove from heat and set aside, covered, until you're ready to combine with other stuffing ingredients.

2. Dry-roast sunflower seeds and cumin in a cast iron frying pan over medium heat, shaking the pan frequently, until seeds are aromatic and begin to crackle, about 5 minutes. Drain any excess liquid, remove from heat and set aside to cool.

3. In a medium bowl, combine the emmer, herbs, onion and garlic, followed by the sunflower and cumin seeds, currants, salt and pepper.

4. In a small bowl, whisk together the sunflower seed butter, olive oil, lemon juice and zest. Add to emmer mixture and mix thoroughly. Set filling aside until you're ready to stuff the leaves.

Continued on page 116

5. Carefully unpack grape leaves from the jar and unroll them. Make two piles—torn leaves and scraps in one pile, and intact leaves and those that can be patched in another. (The torn and unpatchable leaves will be used to line the cooking pot so the stuffed leaves don't stick to the bottom.)

6. Boil a large saucepan of water. Blanch the intact leaves at a rolling boil for 3 minutes. Use tongs to transfer the blanched leaves to a colander. Allow to cool slightly.

7. Prepare a parchment-lined baking sheet. Carefully separate 8 or 9 leaves at a time from the blanched pile and lay them, vein side up, on a clean towel. Snip off any long stems. Patch any holes with scraps of the reserved, torn leaves.

8. Place about 1 tablespoon (15 mL) of filling near the base of each leaf. Fold the base and sides of the leaf over the filling and roll up tightly. Place dolmades on baking sheet. Repeat with the remaining leaves. (You might have leftover filling—freeze for later use in stuffed peppers or zucchini.)

9. Select a large, heavy-bottomed saucepan and a heatproof plate close to the same diameter to fit inside it, for weighing down the dolmades. Select a shallow heatproof bowl to place on top of the plate.

10. Line the bottom of the saucepan with the remaining torn leaves and pieces. Pack the dolmades in the bottom of the pan in a tight circle, starting from the outside and working inward. Create a second layer if necessary. Place the plate over top and the bowl on the plate.

11. Pour over enough vegetable stock to cover the dolmades by 1 inch (2.5 cm). Bring the pot to the boil over medium heat, reduce heat to low and simmer the dolmades for 30 minutes.

12. Carefully remove plate and bowl, and pour stock off into another bowl. Reserve 1 cup (250 mL) stock for the sauce and save the remainder for another use. Transfer dolmades to a warmed serving platter and set aside, uncovered, while you make the Avgolemono Sauce. Serve dolmades on a platter at room temperature with a pitcher of the sauce on the side.

AVGOLEMONO SAUCE

MAKES 1 CUP (250 ML) OF SAUCE.

3 large eggs
¼–½ cup (60–120 mL) lemon juice
(about 2–4 lemons), to taste

1 cup (250 mL) cooking stock
from dolmades
1 Tbsp (15 mL) melted butter
(optional)

1. Fill the bottom of a double boiler with 1 inch (2.5 cm) water. Cover and bring to the boil, then reduce heat so that the water is barely simmering.

2. Before placing the top of the double boiler over the simmering water, crack the eggs into it and beat until light and foamy. Warm the lemon juice for 15 seconds in the microwave (use the larger amount for a sharper flavour) and gradually beat into the eggs.

3. Place the egg-lemon mixture over the barely simmering water and gradually add stock, whisking constantly. Whisk in butter, if using, and stir with a wooden spoon until sauce is thick enough to coat the back of the spoon. Remove from heat.

VARIATION:
Stuffed Lacinato Kale Leaves

MAKES ABOUT 20 SMALL KALE ROLLS.

When grape leaves are hard to find, **lacinato kale** is a good substitute. The filling recipe will make enough for about 20 smallish kale rolls. Don't worry if some of your rolls are bigger than others—they all take the same amount of time to cook.

Select 20 **similar-sized kale leaves**. Slice off the thin ends, finely chop the stems and mix with the filling. Blanch leaves for 2 minutes, then plunge into cold water and pat dry. Roll as with the regular dolmades, then place in a greased 9-inch (22.5-cm) square pan. Pour over **vegetable stock**, cover pan with foil and bake for 45 minutes at 350F (180C).

Mushroom Tarts with Quinoa Crust

MAKES 12 TARTS.

These tarts can be whipped up in just over an hour—a good item to have in the recipe box for when you're suddenly invited to a potluck. To create a less crunchy crust, this recipe uses a larger amount of water than usual when cooking the quinoa. If you still find the crust too crunchy, simply fill the shells and allow the tarts to stand for 15 minutes before serving.

CRUST

1 cup (250 mL) golden and black quinoa

1¼ cups (330 mL) water

1 egg, beaten

½ tsp (2.5 mL) salt

MUSHROOM FILLING

1 Tbsp (15 mL) butter

1 Tbsp (15 mL) olive oil

3½ cups (830 mL) sliced cremini mushrooms (about 12 oz/340 gr)

2 cloves garlic, minced

1 tsp (5 mL) soy sauce

1 large egg, beaten

½ cup (120 mL) grated Parmesan cheese

1 spring onion, halved lengthwise and finely chopped

1 Tbsp (15 mL) 35 percent cream

1 tsp (5 mL) chopped fresh rosemary

1. Rinse quinoa, then place in a small saucepan. Add water, cover and bring to the boil. Reduce heat to low and cook for 15 minutes, or until all the water is absorbed. Remove from heat and let stand, covered, for 15 minutes. Fluff with a fork and cool to room temperature.

2. While quinoa cools, preheat oven to 375F (190C) and lightly grease a standard 12-cup muffin tin.

3. Whisk in beaten egg and salt to cooled quinoa. Press about 1½ tablespoons (22 mL) quinoa into each muffin cup with your fingers or the back of a spoon, moving up the sides about 1 inch (2.5 cm). (You'll have some quinoa left over to add to stir-fries or other cooked dishes.)

Photo courtesy Merinka/Thinkstock

4. Bake for 10 minutes, until tops of crusts are just beginning to brown. Remove from oven and allow to cool slightly before adding filling.

5. Melt butter and oil over medium-high heat in a cast iron frying pan. Add mushrooms and sauté, shaking pan frequently, for 5 to 7 minutes, or until mushrooms begin to brown.

6. Add garlic and soy sauce and cook for 2 more minutes until mushrooms just begin to stick to the pan. Remove from heat and transfer mushrooms to a bowl.

7. Whisk together egg, Parmesan, onion, cream and rosemary. Pour over mushrooms and stir to combine.

8. Spoon filling into the cooked quinoa crusts. Bake tarts for another 15 to 20 minutes, or until filling is bubbly and aromatic. Remove from oven, cool on a rack for 2 to 3 minutes and then remove tarts from cups with the help of a thin-bladed knife or metal spatula. Serve warm or at room temperature.

Buckwheat Blini with Savoury Toppings

MAKES ABOUT SIXTY 1½-INCH (3.8-CM) BLINI, OR 20 TO 25 SERVINGS.

Buckwheat blini could just as easily fit in the breakfast section—if we called them pancakes and made them a few inches bigger. But blini work so well as a flavourful underpinning for savoury toppings that they were voted in as an appetizer recipe instead. Tip: a squeeze bottle with a nozzle top really helps in making the blini a consistent 2-inch (5-cm) size.

1½ cups (350 mL) milk

1 tsp (5 mL) dry active yeast

½ cup (120 mL) organic, unbleached all-purpose flour, divided

½ cup (120 mL) buckwheat flour

¼ tsp (1 mL) salt

1 Tbsp (15 mL) melted butter

2 eggs, separated

Canola or sunflower oil, for pan

1. Heat milk until lukewarm, about 115F (45C). Pour into a medium mixing bowl and stir in yeast and ¼ cup (60 mL) of the all-purpose flour. Let stand until bubbly, about 10 minutes.

2. In a separate bowl, whisk together the remaining all-purpose flour, buckwheat flour and salt. Whisk dry ingredients into the milk mixture until batter is smooth and thick, then whisk in melted butter.

3. Cover batter with plastic wrap and leave at room temperature until doubled in size, from 2 to 3 hours. (At this stage you can refrigerate the batter and continue the next day. Bring the batter to room temperature before proceeding.)

4. Beat egg yolks and whisk into the batter. In a separate bowl, beat egg whites until stiff. Gradually fold into batter.

5. For appetizer-sized blini, pour batter through a funnel into squeeze bottle. Heat a cast iron frying pan or griddle over medium heat. Brush with canola or sunflower oil—just enough to lightly coat the pan. Squeeze batter in small rounds of about 1½ inches (3.8 cm) onto surface of the pan. Cook for 2 minutes, or until bubbles begin to form on the surface. Flip and cook for another minute.

6. For hot canapés, keep each batch warm in a 200F (95C) oven. For cold canapés—and blini are just as good cold—cool cooked blini on a rack. Serve with your favourite combination of toppings. Store extra blini in the fridge for up to 4 days.

Toppings
CHÈVRE AND CHIVES

MAKES ABOUT ½ CUP (120 ML), ENOUGH FOR ABOUT 24 BLINI.

4 oz (110 gr) chèvre
1 Tbsp (15 mL) plain yogurt
   or 10 percent cream

2 Tbsp (30 mL) chopped chives
   (or substitute the green ends of
   green onions)
½ tsp (2.5 mL) freshly ground
   black pepper

1. Mash cheese lightly with a fork and stir in yogurt or cream to a spreadable consistency. Add chives and black pepper and mix thoroughly.

Continued on page 122

QUICK BEET COMPOTE

MAKES ABOUT 3 CUPS (710 ML).

A sweet and tart compote that goes beautifully with chèvre and other cheeses. Try spreading blini with the chèvre-chive mixture and topping with compote.

2 medium beets
I crisp apple such as Ambrosia
I large red onion
I Tbsp (15 mL) olive oil

2 Tbsp (30 mL) balsamic vinegar
I Tbsp (15 mL) maple syrup
I tsp (5 mL) kosher salt

1. Peel beets and grate coarsely. Core apple (without peeling), slice into eighths and slice each eighth crosswise into ¼-inch (0.6-cm) pieces. Set aside.

2. Thinly slice onion lengthwise. Heat oil in a cast iron frying pan over medium heat, add onion and sauté until softened, 10 to 12 minutes.

3. Stir reserved beet and apple into the pan with the onions, followed by the vinegar, maple syrup and salt.

4. Cook just until beets have softened and apples still have a bit of crunch, from 10 to 12 minutes. Remove from heat and cool to room temperature. Store in a covered container in refrigerator for up to 1 week.

OTHER TOPPING SUGGESTIONS:

Kalamata olive tapenade with a slice of baby cucumber
Basil pesto and roasted red peppers
Crème fraîche and watercress

Tomato chutney and candied walnut
Chopped arugula and curls of Norwegian Gjetost cheese
... and of course, whipped cream or crème fraîche and berries

Lime-Scented Green Pea, Coconut Milk and Wheat Berry Soup

MAKES 6 SERVINGS.

A beautiful soup for when the fresh peas are just coming out of the garden. Try grilled flatbread as an accompaniment, or Whole Wheat Chapatis (page 164) hot from the griddle.

2 tsp (10 mL) canola oil

1 medium onion, finely chopped

3 cups (710 mL) fresh or frozen green peas, divided

3 cups (710 mL) vegetable stock

5 lime leaves, or substitute 2 tsp (10 mL) grated lime zest and 3 bay leaves

14-oz (398-mL) can coconut milk

1½ cups (350 mL) cooked wheat berries (emmer, einkorn or Khorasan; see sidebar on page 137 for cooking instructions)

½ cup (120 mL) finely chopped cilantro

½ tsp (2.5 mL) salt

½ tsp (2.5 mL) freshly ground pepper

1. Heat oil in a medium-sized saucepan over medium heat. Add onions and cook for 5 minutes, until softened.

2. Add 2 cups (475 mL) peas, vegetable stock and lime leaves. Increase heat to medium high, bring to the boil, then reduce heat to medium low and simmer for 20 minutes.

3. Remove pan from heat, remove lime leaves from the soup and purée until smooth with an immersion blender or in a food processor. Return pan to burner set at medium low.

4. Stir in coconut milk, remaining 1 cup (250 mL) peas and wheat berries and simmer gently for 10 minutes. Stir in chopped cilantro, salt and pepper. Taste, adjust seasonings if needed and serve immediately.

TIP: Lime leaves can be harder to find in smaller communities. On your next trip to the big city, bring home fresh lime leaves and freeze them. They lose their bright colour but none of their flavour, and they'll brighten up soups and stir-fries for up to a year.

Beet and Cranberry Borscht with Whole Grain Dumplings

MAKES 4 SUBSTANTIAL OR 6 SMALLER SERVINGS.

Truly fluffy dumplings require a bit of strategizing. Make sure the soup is just barely simmering, so that the dumplings steam rather than boil. Scoop the dough with a spoon dipped in hot water—if you compact the dumpling mixture too much it tends to turn into a bullet. Finally, don't crowd the dumplings in the pot, and plan to eat them all when you serve the soup—the dough will not deliver the same fluffiness the next day.

BORSCHT

1 Tbsp (15 mL) olive oil

1 medium onion, finely chopped

2 stalks celery, halved lengthwise and chopped

2 medium carrots, quartered lengthwise and chopped

2 cloves garlic, minced

1 tsp (5 mL) anise seed

1 cup (250 mL) cranberries

1 lb (455 gr) beets (about 2 large) peeled, washed and diced into ½-inch (1.25-cm) pieces

6 cups (1.4 L) vegetable stock

1 lb (455 gr) red potatoes (about 2 large) peeled, washed and diced into ½-inch (1.5-cm) pieces

DUMPLINGS

¾ cup (180 mL) whole wheat cake and pastry flour

¼ cup (60 mL) dark rye flour

½ tsp (2.5 mL) salt

2 tsp (10 mL) baking powder

½ tsp (2.5 mL) fennel or caraway seeds

1 large egg

2 Tbsp (30 mL) milk, plus 1 Tbsp (15 mL) if needed

1. Heat the oil in a large saucepan over medium heat. Sauté onion until softened, about 5 minutes. Stir in the celery, carrots and garlic and sauté for another 3 to 5 minutes. Add the anise seed and the cranberries and cook until the cranberries begin to pop. Stir in the beets, followed by the stock.

2. Bring to the boil, reduce heat and simmer for 30 minutes. Add the potatoes and simmer for another 15 to 20 minutes, or until potatoes are soft.

Above: This Egyptian wheat does very well in the Pacific Northwest. Karen Mouat photo

3. While the soup is simmering, prepare the dumplings. Whisk together the dry ingredients. Beat egg and milk together and stir into dry ingredients with a fork. The dough should be stiff and not too moist. If dough appears too dry, add the extra milk, 1 teaspoon (5 mL) at a time.

4. When you're ready to cook the dumplings, have a small bowl of hot water ready by the stove.

5. Dip a dessert spoon into the hot water and then into the dough, scooping out about 1 tablespoon (15 mL). Drop dough into the simmering soup, using another spoon to help push it off. Continue until the pot is filled with dumplings but not so full they're touching one another—this recipe should make 12 to 16 dumplings.

6. Cover the pot and simmer for 10 minutes. Check for doneness by slicing one dumpling in half—if there's still uncooked dough at the centre, simmer for a few minutes more.

7. Serve immediately, with 3 to 4 dumplings in each bowl.

Barley Congee for Supper

MAKES ABOUT 8 CUPS (1.9 L), ENOUGH FOR 8 SERVINGS.

Congee is a mild porridge found in several Asian cuisines. It's usually made with a small amount of rice cooked in a large amount of water or broth, and served either on its own or with several flavourful side dishes. Though rice is the traditional starch, congee adapts well to different whole grains, from amaranth to barley. Served plain, barley congee is a soothing dish for an invalid; served with highly flavoured vegetables and condiments, it becomes an exciting main course meal.

Hulled barley takes a good 2 to 2½ hours to turn into the porridge-like consistency of congee, but the resulting soft and yet slightly chewy texture and earthy flavour is worth it.

I cup (250 mL) hulled barley
8 cups (I.9 L) water
Salt

1. Rinse barley under running water. Bring water to a boil in a large pot and add barley. Bring to a boil again, cover the pot and turn heat to low. Simmer for 2 to 2½ hours, until congee is thick and barley is very soft. Add salt to taste. Serve with 4 or 5 side dishes at the table, which diners can add to their own bowls in any combination they choose.

Continued on page 130

Suggested Accompaniments

CRISPY GARLIC AND ONIONS

4 large cloves garlic

I large white onion

2 Tbsp (30 mL) vegetable oil

1. Thinly slice whole cloves of garlic lengthwise. Cut onions in half lengthwise and slice thinly from top to bottom.

2. Heat oil in a cast iron frying pan over a burner set between medium and medium high. Test oil for readiness by placing a piece of garlic in the pan—if it sizzles immediately, the oil is ready. Add all the garlic at once and have a slotted spoon ready—it cooks fast. As soon as it changes colour—in about 30 seconds—remove garlic from the oil and drain on paper towel.

3. Add onion to the same oil and cook until brown and crispy—about 3 minutes. Remove onion and drain on paper towel. Place garlic and onions in a small bowl for serving.

SAUTÉED OYSTER MUSHROOMS

8 oz (225 gr) fresh oyster mushrooms, torn into slim lengths

I Tbsp (15 mL) butter

I Tbsp (15 mL) cooking sherry

½ tsp (2.5 mL) kosher salt

1. Start mushrooms in a dry, hot pan over medium-high heat. Cook for 3 to 4 minutes, until mushrooms have released their liquid and are beginning to brown. Stir in butter and toss to coat. Cook for another 2 to 3 minutes, until mushrooms are browned on all sides. Stir in sherry, and when it has evaporated, add salt, tossing mushrooms once more. Remove from heat and place in a small bowl for serving.

SAUTÉED MUSTARD OR OTHER PEPPERY GREENS

I Tbsp (15 mL) olive oil

8 oz (225 gr) mustard greens, washed and roughly chopped

I Tbsp (15 mL) apple cider vinegar

½ tsp (2.5 mL) kosher salt

1. Heat oil in a cast iron frying pan over medium heat. When it's hot, add the greens and sauté for 3 to 5 minutes, until wilted and just beginning to brown. Stir in the vinegar and, once it has evaporated, add the salt and toss. Remove from heat and place in a small bowl for serving.

CHOPPED FRESH CILANTRO

2 cups (475 mL) cilantro leaves, cleaned and stemmed

1. Chop cilantro roughly and transfer to a small serving bowl.

TOASTED SLICED ALMONDS

½ cup (120 mL) sliced almonds

1. Dry-roast almonds in a cast iron frying pan for 5 minutes, until aromatic and beginning to brown. Let cool and transfer to a small bowl.

OTHER SUGGESTIONS AND SUBSTITUTIONS

1. The sky's the limit, but try roasted peanuts; deep-fried tofu; chopped Thai basil; cooked arame tossed with rice vinegar, soy sauce and sesame seeds; lemon or lime juice; a fried egg…

2. Fill small bowls with condiments such as Vegetarian Fish Sauce (page 145) and Sambal Oelek to serve alongside the toppings.

Soybean Fasolada Sopa

MAKES 4 TO 5 GENEROUS SERVINGS.

Soybeans give a meatier flavour to this Greek classic. They do take longer to cook than the usual small white beans, though, so cook the beans by themselves for an hour before adding the other ingredients. *Vegan*, IF YOU SKIP THE GREEK YOGURT

1 cup (250 mL) dry soybeans
5–6 cups (1.2–1.4 L) water
3 Tbsp (45 mL) olive oil, divided
1 medium onion, finely chopped
2 cloves garlic, minced
1 medium carrot, quartered lengthwise and chopped

1 tsp (5 mL) dried oregano
2 Tbsp (30 mL) tomato paste
¼ cup (60 mL) finely chopped parsley, divided
1 large fresh field tomato, coarsely chopped
4 Tbsp (60 mL) Greek yogurt, for serving

1. The night before you make the soup, rinse the soybeans, cover with water in a medium pot and let soak overnight.

2. Drain soybeans. In a medium saucepan, cover beans with water by 1 inch (2.5 cm). Cover the pot and bring to the boil, then reduce heat and simmer for 1 hour.

3. Meanwhile, place 1 tablespoon (15 mL) of the olive oil in a separate skillet over medium heat. Sauté the onions until softened, about 5 minutes. Add the garlic and carrots and sauté for another 2 to 3 minutes, then stir in oregano and tomato paste.

4. When the beans have cooked for 1 hour, stir in the onion mixture along with the remaining 2 Tbsp (30 mL) olive oil and continue to simmer until beans are soft, about 1 more hour.

5. When beans are cooked, remove about 1 cup (250 mL) of the soup and purée in a blender. Add back to the soup with half the parsley and all of the chopped tomato. Cook for a further 10 minutes to allow tomato to soften and flavours to blend.

6. Serve in bowls with a tablespoon (15 mL) of Greek yogurt and a sprinkling of parsley over top of each portion.

Buckwheat and Soybean Salad with Lemon-Parsley Vinaigrette

MAKES 6 SERVINGS.

Buckwheat and soybeans provide the substance, fresh vegetables the crunch, and parsley and lemon the brightness in this delightful side salad.

SALAD

1 cup (250 mL) buckwheat groats

1 cup (250 mL) water

2 cups (475 mL) cooked soybeans

1½ cups (350 mL) grated carrot

2 stalks celery, thinly sliced on the diagonal

½ medium red onion, thinly sliced

½ red pepper, thinly sliced into 1-inch (2.5-cm) lengths

A handful of fresh sprouts of your choice, roughly chopped (for instructions, see Chapter 11, pages 91–92)

VINAIGRETTE

2 cups (475 mL) packed parsley, washed and stemmed

2 cloves garlic

½ cup (120 mL) fresh lemon juice (2 juicy lemons)

Zest of 2 lemons

1 tsp (5 mL) Sambal Oelek

1 tsp (5 mL) kosher salt

1 tsp (5 mL) freshly ground pepper

½ cup (120 mL) olive oil

Lemon wedges, for serving

1. Dry-roast the buckwheat groats in a cast iron frying pan set over medium heat for 5 to 7 minutes, or until lightly browned and aromatic. Transfer to a small saucepan. Add water, bring to the boil, reduce heat and simmer for 5 minutes.

2. Buckwheat groats can get clumpy, through no fault of the cook's. To separate them, line a baking sheet with parchment. Fluff groats with a fork, then transfer to the baking sheet, spreading them out with a fork or spatula. Cool to room temperature. With clean hands, rub groats lightly through your fingers, breaking up any lumps. Transfer to a salad bowl.

3. Add remaining salad ingredients to the groats and toss lightly together.

4. To make vinaigrette, place parsley and garlic in the bowl of a food processor and pulse until thoroughly minced. Add lemon juice, lemon zest, Sambal Oelek, salt and pepper and pulse again to combine. Pour in oil in a steady stream while the machine is running.

5. Pour vinaigrette over salad and toss together. Serve with a wedge of lemon on the side.

Poké Bowl with Whole Grains, Edamame Beans and Marinated Tofu

MAKES 4 SERVINGS.

Poké bowls give us a chance to show off our latent food styling skills—they're easy to make beautiful and so, so delicious. This one celebrates all the good things that come out of the garden—mix and match with whatever you've got growing this season. Admittedly, that might not be avocado in our northerly climes. But since we're in the tropics already with this traditional Hawaiian dish, consider adding a few slices of tropical fruit, in season.

DRESSING

¼ cup (60 mL) olive oil

¼ cup (60 mL) rice vinegar

¼ cup (60 mL) lemon or lime juice

2 Tbsp (30 mL) toasted pumpkin seed oil

2 Tbsp (30 mL) toasted sesame seed oil

2 Tbsp (30 mL) soy sauce

2 Tbsp (30 mL) maple syrup

2 tsp (10 mL) minced fresh ginger

MARINATED TOFU

1 clove garlic, minced

1 tsp (5 mL) Sambal Oelek

1 block firm tofu, cut into bite-sized cubes

SALAD

2 cups (475 mL) cooked whole grain of your choice

2 cups (475 mL) cooked edamame (fresh or frozen; for cooking instructions, see How to Enjoy Soybeans, page 75)

2 cups (475 mL) arugula

1 cup (250 mL) halved and sliced cucumber

2 avocados, pitted and sliced

4 red radishes, thinly sliced

½ cup (120 mL) sprouts of your choice

TOPPINGS

1 green onion, finely sliced on the diagonal

2 Tbsp (30 mL) toasted flaxseeds

7-spice blend (shichimi togarashi)

2 Tbsp (30 mL) crumbled Nori seaweed

½ cup (120 mL) sliced Vidalia onion

Continued on page 136

POKÉ BOWL WITH WHOLE GRAINS, EDAMAME BEANS AND MARINATED TOFU CONTINUED

1. Whisk dressing ingredients together in a medium bowl. Set aside one-half to dress the salad.

2. Whisk garlic and Sambal Oelek into the remaining dressing mixture in a medium bowl. Toss tofu cubes in dressing, cover and refrigerate for 1 to 2 hours.

3. In 4 deep serving bowls, arrange grains, edamame and arugula in a rough triangle. Top with sliced cucumber, avocado, marinated tofu and radish, ending with sprouts.

4. Sprinkle each serving with toppings and pour reserved dressing around and overtop. Serve immediately.

Photo courtesy merc67/Thinkstock

Khorasan, Cucumber and Apple Salad with Lemon-Yogurt Vinaigrette

MAKES 6 SERVINGS.

This bright and tangy salad is a great lunch on its own but a wonderful side dish to accompany vegetable curry and dhal for dinner too.

3 cups (710 mL) cooked whole Khorasan (kamut; see sidebar below for cooking instructions)

½ English cucumber, quartered and thinly sliced

1 small red onion, thinly sliced

1 crisp, firm apple, cored, cut into eighths and thinly sliced

1 cup (250 mL) loosely packed mint leaves, chopped

VINAIGRETTE

⅓ cup (80 mL) fresh lemon juice (about 2 lemons)

Grated zest of 1 lemon

2 Tbsp (30 mL) olive oil

¾ cup (180 mL) plain yogurt

1 tsp (5 mL) kosher salt

1. Combine Khorasan, cucumber, onion, apple and mint in a salad bowl and toss well.

2. In a small bowl, whisk vinaigrette ingredients together. Pour over salad and toss. Serve right away or after chilling for a couple of hours in the refrigerator. The salad will keep for a couple of days in the fridge but is best the first day.

How to Cook Wheat Berries

To cook **emmer, einkorn** or other **wheat berries,** use a ratio of 1 part grain to 2 parts water. Rinse the grain first, then add to boiling water, cover, bring back to a boil, reduce heat and simmer for 40 to 50 minutes, checking after 40 minutes. Grains from different sources may take more or less time to cook. If the grain is cooked but still chewy, and you like the texture, simply drain off excess water. One cup (250 mL) of raw grain and two cups (475 mL) of water will make three cups (710 mL) of cooked grain.

Quinoa and Amaranth Salad with Roasted Root Vegetables, Green Onions and Blood Orange

MAKES 6 SERVINGS.

Earthy black amaranth and roasted root vegetables are a good match in this winter salad. Blood oranges and a citrus vinaigrette add a bit of brightness to those dark January days. Tip: Cook more beets and turnips than you need for this salad, and pack them for lunch or use in other recipes.

2 medium-sized white and purple turnips

2 Tbsp (30 mL) olive oil, divided

2 Tbsp (30 mL) apple cider vinegar, divided

1 tsp (5 mL) kosher salt, divided

2 bunches green onions

3 medium-sized beets

2 blood oranges

2 cups (475 mL) cooked quinoa (for cooking instructions, see How to Enjoy Quinoa Seed, page 64)

1½ cups (350 mL) cooked black amaranth (for cooking instructions, see How to Enjoy Amaranth Seed, page 22)

1 cup (250 mL) Candied Nuts and Seeds (see recipe on page 140)

VINAIGRETTE

2 Tbsp (30 mL) lemon juice

¼ cup (60 mL) olive oil

½ tsp (2.5 mL) kosher salt

½ tsp (2.5 mL) freshly ground black pepper

1 tsp (5 mL) Sambal Oelek

1. Preheat oven to 400F (205C) and line 3 baking sheets with parchment.

2. Trim and peel turnips and cut each one into 4 to 6 wedges. Toss with 1 tablespoon (15 mL) each of the olive oil and apple cider vinegar and ½ teaspoon (2.5 mL) of the salt. Transfer to a baking sheet, setting the bowl to one side.

3. Trim and clean onions and cut on the diagonal into 1-inch (2.5-cm) lengths. Transfer to the same bowl used for the turnips and toss in the oil, vinegar and salt remaining in the bottom of the bowl. Transfer to a baking sheet.

Continued on page 140

4. Trim beets and cook them, unpeeled, in simmering water for 30 minutes. Drain, cover beets with cold water and peel. Cut each beet
into 4 to 6 wedges. Toss with remaining tablespoon (15 mL) each of oil
and vinegar and ½ teaspoon (2.5 mL) salt and transfer to a baking sheet.

5. Roast vegetables. Remove onions after 15 minutes and turnips and beets
after 30 minutes. Cool to room temperature. Slice wedges of beets and
turnips crosswise into triangles. Set aside.

6. Zest the blood oranges, then peel and cut into small wedges, setting the
peels and zest aside. Combine cooked grains in a medium bowl, tossing
with 2 forks to break up any lumps. Stir in vegetables, orange wedges and
zest. Squeeze any juice from the reserved orange peels over top.

7. Whisk the vinaigrette ingredients together. Toss salad with half the vinaigrette, taste and add more if needed. Toss the candied nuts and seeds in
at the end. Serve immediately.

CANDIED NUTS AND SEEDS

MAKES ABOUT 1 CUP (250 ML).

This recipe calls for quick action, so be sure to assemble
everything you need before starting. The candied nuts and seeds
are great snacks on the trail, too.

1½ Tbsp (22 mL) brown sugar	½ cup (120 mL) whole pecans
2 tsp (10 mL) water	6 Tbsp (90 mL) sunflower seeds
¼ tsp (1 mL) kosher salt	2 Tbsp (30 mL) sesame seeds

1. Whisk sugar, water and salt into a slurry and place it near the stove, ready
for when you need it. Heat a cast iron frying pan over medium heat.

2. When pan is hot, add pecans and seeds and dry-roast for about 3 minutes,
shaking pan frequently. As soon as the nuts are aromatic and beginning
to brown, add the brown sugar mixture. Quickly stir to coat the nuts. The
sugar burns easily, so as soon it starts to sizzle, after 15 to 20 seconds,
remove pan from heat. The sugar will harden almost immediately.

3. Cool to room temperature before adding to salad.

Whole Grain Tabbouleh with Toasted Walnuts and Feta

MAKES 6 TO 8 SERVINGS.

This close relative of the Lebanese classic goes very well with a side of grilled Portobello mushrooms.

I cup (250 mL) chopped toasted walnuts

3 cups (710 mL) cooked whole grain of your choice

1½ cups (350 mL) diced tomatoes (2 to 3 medium)

1½ cups (350 mL) diced, unpeeled English cucumber (about ⅓ large cucumber)

I cup (250 mL) diced red onion (about I medium)

I cup (250 mL) packed, chopped fresh parsley

½ cup (120 mL) packed, chopped fresh mint

I cup (250 mL) crumbled feta cheese

VINAIGRETTE

⅓ cup (80 mL) lemon juice (about 2 lemons)

⅓ cup (80 mL) olive oil

2 cloves garlic, minced

½ tsp (2.5 mL) salt

½ tsp (2.5 mL) pepper

1. Line a baking sheet with parchment paper and preheat the oven to 350F (180C).

2. Spread walnuts on baking sheet and toast for 7 to 8 minutes, or until aromatic. Cool to room temperature, then toss walnuts and remaining salad ingredients together in a medium bowl.

3. Whisk vinaigrette ingredients together, pour over salad and toss gently. Refrigerate for a couple of hours before serving. Salad keeps well for several days.

Khorasan, Chickpea and Eggplant Salad

MAKES 6 GENEROUS SERVINGS.

Chickpeas, eggplant, preserved lemons and harissa sauce—can you guess we're travelling to the Middle East? Preserved lemons can be difficult to find, but they're easy to make at home—it just takes a bit of planning ahead so they're ready when you need them. *Vegan* IF YOU SKIP THE CHÈVRE

I large eggplant (about I lb/455 gr]), cut into small cubes

3 Tbsp (45 mL) olive oil, divided

½ tsp (2.5 mL) kosher salt

I tsp (5 mL) ground, toasted cumin

¼ tsp (I mL) cinnamon

I large red pepper, seeded and cut into 8

I large preserved lemon (see sidebar opposite or purchase from a Middle Eastern specialty store)

3 cups (475 mL) cooked Khorasan

⅓ cup (80 mL) oily sun-dried olives, pitted and chopped

I red habanero pepper, seeded and minced

2 cups (475 mL) cooked chickpeas

½ cup (120 mL) packed, chopped cilantro

6 oz (170 gr) soft chèvre

VINAIGRETTE

¼ cup (60 mL) olive oil

¼ cup (60 mL) fresh lemon juice (about I lemon)

I Tbsp (15 mL) Quick Harissa Sauce (see recipe opposite)

1. Preheat oven to 400F (205C) and line 2 baking sheets with parchment.

2. Toss eggplant cubes in 2 tablespoons (30 mL) of the oil, ½ tsp (2.5 mL) salt, and the cumin and cinnamon. Place on a baking sheet. Toss red pepper pieces with remaining tablespoon (15 mL) oil and a pinch of salt and place on the second baking sheet.

3. Roast vegetables for 20 to 30 minutes, until eggplant is browned and soft inside, and peppers are lightly blackened and soft. Remove from oven and cool to room temperature, then roughly chop the peppers.

4. Remove flesh and seeds from lemon and discard. Slice each lemon segment crosswise into thin strips. Combine lemon, eggplant, red pepper and remaining salad ingredients except for the chèvre in a salad bowl.

5. Whisk oil, lemon juice and harissa together. Toss salad with vinaigrette. Break chèvre into small pieces, add to salad and gently toss again. Serve at room temperature.

QUICK HARISSA SAUCE

MAKES ABOUT ⅓ CUP (80 ML).

There are many versions of this fiery Middle Eastern and North African condiment. This one is quick and easy.

1 tsp (5 mL) cumin seeds
1 tsp (5 mL) fennel seeds
1 Tbsp (30 mL) dried crushed
   red peppers

3 cloves garlic
¼ tsp (1 mL) kosher salt
¼ cup (60 mL) olive oil
2 tsp (10 mL) lemon juice

1. Dry-roast cumin and fennel seeds in a cast iron frying pan over medium heat until aromatic and beginning to pop, about 5 minutes. Remove from heat and allow to cool for about 5 minutes.

2. Coarsely grind spices, garlic and salt in a mortar and pestle or food processor. In a small bowl or food processor, whisk or pulse in olive oil and lemon juice to make a thick paste. Store in a small jar in the refrigerator. Will keep for up to 1 month.

Preserved Lemons

MAKES 2 PRESERVED LEMONS.

Adapted from Paula Wolfert's *The Slow Mediterranean Kitchen*

2 organic lemons, washed and
   well dried
⅓ cup (80 mL) coarse or kosher salt

½ cup (120 mL) fresh lemon juice

Cut each lemon into 8 wedges and toss with the salt. Place wedges in a 1-cup (250-mL) jar and pour in fresh lemon juice, pressing with a wooden spoon to make sure the juice penetrates to the bottom. It's best to seal the jar with a plastic lid, but if using a metal lid, place a piece of waxed paper over the jar first.

Leave the lemons at room temperature, shaking the jar every day to distribute the juice and salt. The lemons will be ready to use after 7 days, and can be stored in the fridge for another week. Rinse before using and pat dry.

Vietnamese-Inspired Red Quinoa, Arugula and Mushroom Salad

SERVES 4 AS A MAIN COURSE OR 6 AS A SIDE DISH.

Who knew that Vegetarian Fish Sauce was within our grasp? Vegans who once ate fish are particular fans of this salad.

¼ cup (60 mL) black sesame seeds

2 cups (475 mL) arugula

1½ Tbsp (22 mL) vegetable oil

6 oz (170 gr) shiitake
  mushrooms, sliced

4 oz (110 gr) cremini
  mushrooms, sliced

2 tsp (10 mL) soy sauce

2 cups (475 mL) cooked red or black
  quinoa (for cooking instructions,
  see How to Enjoy Quinoa
  Seed, page 64)

2 spring onions, thinly sliced on
  the diagonal

1 cup (250 mL) grated carrot
  (about 1 medium)

1 stick celery, thinly sliced on
  the diagonal

½ cup (120 mL) packed, chopped
  fresh cilantro

½ cup (120 mL) packed, chopped
  fresh mint

DRESSING

3 Tbsp (45 mL) lemon juice

1½ Tbsp (22 mL) maple syrup

2 Tbsp (30 mL) Vegetarian Fish Sauce
  (see recipe opposite)

1 tsp (5 mL) Sambal Oelek

1 clove garlic, minced

1 Tbsp (15 mL) toasted
  sesame seed oil

1. Dry-roast sesame seeds in a cast iron frying pan over medium heat for 5 minutes, shaking pan occasionally, or until seeds begin to crackle. Pour seeds into a salad bowl.

2. Rinse arugula and, without drying, chop roughly (if using baby arugula, no need to chop). Add to the sesame pan without oil and quickly cook until just wilted, about 2 minutes. Add to salad bowl.

3. Heat oil in the same pan, still over medium heat, and add mushrooms, stirring and shaking the pan to coat mushrooms with oil. Cook for 5 minutes, or until just beginning to brown. Add soy sauce, stir, and cook for another 1 minute. Remove from heat and set aside.

4. Add cooked quinoa and remaining vegetables (but not the mushrooms) and herbs to the salad bowl and whisk dressing ingredients together. Toss salad with 3 to 4 tablespoons (45 to 60 mL) of dressing, taste and add more dressing if necessary. Divide salad between 4 heated bowls and spoon mushrooms over top. Serve at once.

VEGETARIAN FISH SAUCE

MAKES ABOUT 1½ CUPS (350 ML).

This sauce provides a fierce, briny jolt of umami to Asian-inspired dishes, and is an utterly convincing substitute for authentic fish sauce. Though it seems outlandish to use 2 whole tablespoons (30 mL) of salt, the result is spectacular.

I large clove garlic, crushed

I oz (30 gr) dried shiitake mushrooms

⅓ cup (80 mL) soy sauce

2 Tbsp (30 mL) salt

I cup (250 mL) hijiki or
   arame seaweed

3 cups (710 mL) water

1. Combine all ingredients in a medium saucepan. Cover and bring to a boil over high heat. Reduce heat to low, remove cover and simmer until liquid is reduced by half. Strain through a fine-meshed sieve, reserving vegetables to make stock. Cool sauce to room temperature, pour into a glass jar and store in the refrigerator for up to 3 weeks.

Bonus Stock

Add whatever kitchen scraps you have on hand—carrot, celery or onion scraps, the stems from mint and cilantro, mushroom ends—to the boiled shiitake mushrooms and seaweed in a saucepan. Add cold water to cover. Bring to a boil, reduce heat to medium low, uncover and simmer for I hour. You will have a deeply flavoured stock that will add oomph to any grain or bean dish.

Red or Black Quinoa Greek Salad

MAKES 6 GENEROUS SERVINGS.

Coloured quinoa is just more dramatic somehow. Note that there's no vinegar in this salad—ripe, juicy tomatoes provide all the acid you'll need. This salad will not suffer from being made an hour or two before you're ready to serve—it will give the tomatoes time to release some of their juices.

2 cups (475 mL) cooked red or black quinoa (for cooking instructions, see How to Enjoy Quinoa Seed, page 64)

2 large, ripe field tomatoes, chopped into chunks

⅓ of an English cucumber, halved lengthwise and chopped

½ large red pepper, thinly sliced

½ red onion, thinly sliced lengthwise

I Tbsp (I5 mL) chopped fresh oregano

I–I½ cups (250–350 mL) crumbled feta cheese, to taste

I cup (250 mL) Kalamata olives, unpitted

⅓ cup (80 mL) olive oil

Kosher salt and ground pepper to taste

1. Layer ingredients in a large salad bowl and pour olive oil over top. Season with salt and pepper, toss and serve immediately, or refrigerate for 1 to 2 hours before tossing and serving.

Triticale, Leek and Cabbage Colcannon

MAKES 4 GENEROUS SERVINGS.

Triticale takes over from the more traditional potato in this hearty Irish supper dish. Even potato lovers will appreciate the chewy texture contributed by the whole triticale grains.

2 leeks
2 tsp (10 mL) fenugreek seeds
1 Tbsp (15 mL) butter
1 Tbsp (15 mL) olive oil
2 cloves garlic, roughly chopped
4 cups (1 L) roughly chopped green cabbage (about 1 lb/455 gr)
2 Tbsp (30 mL) white wine

2 cups (475 mL) cooked whole triticale grains, or whole wheat grain of your choice (see sidebar on page 161)
1 cup (250 mL) grated sharp cheddar cheese
1 cup (250 mL) 2 percent milk
½ tsp (2.5 mL) salt
½ tsp (2.5 mL) freshly ground pepper
½ cup (120 mL) grated Parmesan cheese

1. Preheat oven to 350F (180C) and lightly grease a 9-inch (22.5-cm) square baking dish.

2. Slice leeks in half lengthwise, slice into pieces crosswise and soak in cold water for 10 minutes. Lift leek pieces into a colander to drain, then shake dry.

3. Sauté fenugreek seeds in butter and oil in a large frying pan set over medium heat for 2 to 3 minutes, or until aromatic. Stir in leeks and cook for 5 to 6 minutes until softened. Add garlic and cook for 2 minutes. Stir in cabbage, followed by white wine. Cover and cook for 7 to 8 minutes, until cabbage is softened.

4. Stir in cooked triticale, cheddar cheese, milk, salt and pepper. Transfer to baking dish. Sprinkle Parmesan cheese evenly over top, and bake for 35 to 40 minutes, until browned and bubbling. Let sit for 5 minutes before serving. Accompany with a simple green salad and some crusty bread.

Roasted Cauliflower, Barley and Hazelnut Pilaf

MAKES 6 TO 8 MAIN COURSE SERVINGS.

A good-quality garam masala is the cook's best friend in making this highly aromatic, Southeast Asian–inspired supper dish. Try grinding your own spice mixture for the freshest possible flavour.

1 cup (250 mL) hulled barley, rinsed and drained

1 cup (250 mL) raw hazelnuts

2 Tbsp (30 mL) unsalted butter

3 Tbsp (45 mL) canola oil, divided

1½ tsp (7.5 mL) cumin seeds

1 bay leaf or curry leaf

1½ tsp (7.5 mL) black mustard seeds

1½ tsp (7.5 mL) ground cardamom

1 cup (250 mL) finely chopped onion (about 1 small)

1-inch (2.5-cm) piece of ginger root, peeled and minced

2 cloves garlic, minced

3 cups (710 mL) water

1 medium head of cauliflower (about 1.5 lbs/680 gr)

2 Tbsp (30 mL) good-quality garam masala

½ tsp (2.5 mL) salt

¼ cup (60 mL) fresh lemon juice (about 1 juicy lemon)

1½ cups (350 mL) chopped fresh cilantro, divided

1. Preheat oven to 350F (180C).

2. Set a cast iron frying pan over medium heat and dry-roast the barley for 5 to 6 minutes, until it stops smelling like wet hay and takes on a nutty aroma. Remove from heat and set aside.

3. Meanwhile, roast hazelnuts in oven for 10 minutes, just until they start to brown. Remove from oven, cool to room temperature, rub with a towel to remove skins and coarsely chop (don't worry if you can't remove all the skin). Increase oven temperature to 400F (205C).

4. Melt butter and 1 tablespoon (15 mL) oil over medium heat in a medium saucepan. Stir in cumin, bay leaf, mustard seeds and cardamom and sauté for 3 to 4 minutes, until seeds begin to pop. Add onion, ginger and garlic and sauté for another 3 to 4 minutes, until onion begins to soften.

Above: The seeds of Excelsior barley are the same colour as the heads. *Karen Mouat photo*

5. Stir cooked barley into onion and spice mixture. Add water, then cover, bring to a boil and reduce heat to low. Simmer for 45 to 50 minutes, until barley is soft but still chewy. Remove from heat, fluff with a fork and let stand, covered, until ready to combine with remaining ingredients.

6. While barley cooks, prepare cauliflower. Break or cut cauliflower into small florets. Whisk 2 tablespoons (30 mL) oil, garam masala and salt together in a medium bowl. Toss cauliflower in the oil mixture and spread out on a parchment-lined baking sheet. Roast for 30 minutes, or until edges are browned.

7. Combine roasted cauliflower with barley mixture in a large bowl and stir in the lemon juice. Toss in hazelnuts and 1 cup (250 mL) of the cilantro. Serve on warmed plates, sprinkling each serving with the remaining cilantro. Accompany with a cucumber raita, steamed greens and Whole Wheat Chapatis with Toasted Flaxseeds (page 164).

Roasted Barley and Morel Mushroom Risotto

MAKES 6 GENEROUS SERVINGS.

Roasted barley and wild morel mushrooms provide a warming family meal for a blustery fall day. Hulled barley takes longer to cook than the traditional Arborio rice; count on 45 to 50 minutes.

1 cup (250 mL) water

1 oz (30 gr) dried morel mushrooms

1 cup (250 mL) hulled barley

1 leek, white and light green parts only

3 Tbsp (45 mL) butter, divided

1 Tbsp (15 mL) olive oil, divided

3 cloves minced garlic, divided

3 cups (710 mL) vegetable stock, divided

1 tsp (5 mL) soy sauce

½ cup (120 mL) plus 1 Tbsp (15 mL) white wine, divided

1 cup (250 mL) grated Parmesan cheese

1. Bring water to a boil, pour over morels and soak mushrooms for 20 minutes.

2. Rinse barley in a sieve and shake off excess water. Transfer to a 10-inch (25-cm) sauté pan with 3-inch (7.5-cm) sides and a close-fitting cover. Dry-roast barley over medium heat for 5 minutes, until aromatic. Pour into a bowl and set aside.

3. Slice leek in half lengthwise, slice into pieces crosswise and soak in cold water for several minutes. Lift leek pieces into a colander to drain, then shake dry.

4. In the same pan, melt 2 tablespoons (30 mL) butter with ½ tablespoon (7.5 mL) oil over medium heat. Add leek and sauté for 5 minutes, until beginning to soften. Add 2 cloves of the garlic and sauté for another 2 minutes. Add roasted barley, stir to coat, and add 2 cups (475 mL) of vegetable stock. Cover, reduce heat to medium low and cook for 15 minutes, or until all the liquid is absorbed.

Photo courtesy bhofack2/Thinkstock

5. Meanwhile, remove morels from their soaking liquid, squeezing them to release excess moisture. Pour soaking liquid into a bowl through a fine-meshed sieve and set aside. Slice morels lengthwise and then crosswise into bite-sized pieces.

6. In a small frying pan, melt remaining tablespoon (15 mL) butter with ½ tablespoon (7.5 mL) oil over medium heat. Sauté morels until aromatic, about 2 to 3 minutes, then add remaining 1 clove of garlic and soy sauce and cook for another 1 minute. Add 1 tablespoon (15 mL) white wine and continue cooking until liquid has evaporated. Remove from heat and set aside.

7. Whisk together the remaining 1 cup (250 mL) stock, ½ cup (120 mL) white wine and the morel soaking liquid. Add liquid to barley ½ cup (120 mL) at a time, covering the pan between additions. It should take about 5 minutes for each addition to be fully absorbed.

8. Once all the liquid has been absorbed and the barley is fully cooked with a creamy but still chewy texture, stir in reserved mushrooms and Parmesan cheese. Serve at once.

Beet and Triticale Gnocchi with Kale Pesto

MAKES 4 SERVINGS.

If you have leftover roasted beets on hand, gnocchi are a delicious way to use them up. Sautéing the cooked gnocchi in butter and oil adds flavour and a tiny bit of caramelizing.

2 medium beets
2 Tbsp (30 mL) olive oil, divided
¾ tsp (4 mL) salt, divided
I large egg, beaten
¼ cup (60 mL) crumbled feta cheese

¼ tsp (I mL) freshly grated nutmeg
2 cups (475 mL) whole triticale flour
(if you can't find triticale flour,
substitute Red Fife)
I Tbsp (I5 mL) butter

1. Preheat oven to 400F (205C) and line a baking sheet with parchment.

2. Trim beets and cook them, unpeeled, in simmering water for 30 minutes. Drain, cover beets with cold water and peel. Cut each beet into 4 to 6 wedges. Toss with 1 tablespoon (15 mL) oil and ½ teaspoon salt (2.5 mL) and transfer to baking sheet. Roast beets for 30 minutes. Cool to room temperature, then roughly chop.

3. Purée roasted beets in a food processor until only very small pieces remain. Add egg, cheese, remaining ¼ tsp (1 mL) salt and nutmeg and purée until smooth.

4. Transfer beet purée to a medium bowl and stir in flour, mixing thoroughly. Tip dough out onto a lightly floured work surface. Knead dough briefly and form into a smooth circle. Cover with plastic wrap and refrigerate for 45 minutes to 1 hour.

5. Line two baking sheets with parchment paper. On a lightly floured surface, divide dough into 4 pieces. Roll each piece into a long rope of about ¾ inch (2 cm) in diameter, pressing lightly but firmly to eliminate cracks in the dough.

6. Cut each rope into ¾-inch (2-cm) pieces. Roll pieces lightly on the work surface to make a rough oblong. To make the characteristic grooves in the gnocchi, pull each piece toward you along the work surface with the tines of a fork. Place finished gnocchi on the parchment-lined baking sheets.

7. When you're ready to cook the gnocchi, boil a large pot of water. Once it is boiling rapidly, reduce heat to medium high for a rolling boil, and with a slotted spoon, lower about 20 gnocchi into the water.

8. Once the gnocchi have cooked they will rise to the surface, after about 2 or 3 minutes. At that point, remove them with a slotted spoon and place on a parchment-lined baking sheet. Continue to cook remaining gnocchi in batches of about 20 at a time.

9. Melt butter with remaining tablespoon (15 mL) olive oil in a frying pan set over medium heat. Sauté gnocchi in batches for 1 or 2 minutes per side, transferring to warmed plates as each serving is ready.

10. Toss gently with Kale Pesto (see recipe below) thinned with a couple of tablespoons (30 mL) of gnocchi cooking water, and serve at once.

KALE PESTO

MAKES ABOUT 1½ CUPS (350 ML).

2 cups (475 mL) chopped Lacinato kale (4 to 5 leaves)

2 large cloves garlic

½ cup (120 mL) pumpkin seeds

2 Tbsp (30 mL) pumpkin seed oil

¼ cup (60 mL) olive oil

1 Tbsp (15 mL) lemon juice

1 tsp (5 mL) soy sauce

½ tsp (2.5 mL) salt

¼ tsp (1 mL) freshly ground pepper

⅓ cup (80 mL) crumbled feta cheese

1. Purée kale and garlic in a food processor. Add pumpkin seeds and purée until smooth. While machine is running, add pumpkin and olive oils, followed by remaining ingredients. Add the feta cheese last, pulsing a couple of times to thoroughly blend in the cheese. Transfer to a container with a lid and refrigerate until ready to use. Will keep for up to 1 week.

Lentil, Einkorn and Nut Terrine with Miso Gravy

MAKES 6 TO 8 SERVINGS OF 2 SLICES EACH.

This beautifully textured, flavourful terrine, served with Miso Gravy, is an excellent vegan main course for traditional holiday feasts. Cold terrine is also delicious in sandwiches with Dijon mustard, arugula and avocado slices. Don't be daunted by the long list of ingredients; once the vegetables are sautéed you just mix everything together in one bowl.

½ cup (120 mL) brown lentils, rinsed and picked through

1 cup (250 mL) water

1 cup (250 mL) finely diced onion

1 Tbsp (15 mL) olive oil

2 large cloves garlic, minced

1 cup (250 mL) chopped celery

1 cup (250 mL) chopped red pepper

1 Tbsp (15 mL) apple cider vinegar

1 Tbsp (15 mL) soy sauce

2 tsp (10 mL) Sambal Oelek or other hot sauce

1 tsp (5 mL) dried rosemary

1 tsp (5 mL) dried thyme

½ tsp (2.5 mL) salt

½ tsp (2.5 mL) pepper

1 cup (250 mL) cooked whole einkorn grains (see sidebar on page 137 for cooking instructions)

1½ cups (350 mL) chopped Brazil nuts

1½ cups (350 mL) chopped cashews

½ cup (120 mL) nutritional yeast

3 flax eggs (see sidebar on page 102)

1. Preheat oven to 350F (180C) and oil a 9 × 5-inch (22.5 × 13-cm) loaf pan.

2. Combine lentils and water in a medium pot. Bring to a rapid boil, then reduce to a gentle simmer. Cover and cook until very tender, almost mushy, 30 to 35 minutes. Remove from heat, mash lightly with a fork and set aside to cool slightly.

3. Sauté onion in olive oil over medium heat for 5 to 7 minutes, or until translucent. Add garlic, celery and red pepper and sauté for another 3 to 4 minutes, until softened. Stir in vinegar, soy sauce, Sambal Oelek and seasonings and cook for 2 minutes more to blend flavours.

4. Remove vegetable mixture from heat and allow to cool for a few minutes.

Mix lentils, grains, nuts and yeast in a large bowl. Add vegetable mixture and flax eggs and stir to combine thoroughly.

5. Press mixture into loaf pan and cover with an oiled piece of parchment paper. Place another loaf pan filled with 1 inch (2.5 cm) of water on top of the parchment paper to weigh down the terrine, then place the whole structure in a larger baking pan and fill the large pan with water until it reaches halfway up the bottom loaf pan.

6. Bake for 35 minutes, then remove the top loaf pan and parchment and bake for another 15 minutes, until terrine is lightly browned on top and has shrunk away from sides of pan. Cool terrine on a rack for 10 minutes before cutting into slices. Serve with Miso Gravy (see recipe below).

MISO GRAVY

MAKES JUST OVER 2 CUPS (475 ML).

2 Tbsp (30 mL) olive oil

3 Tbsp (45 mL) whole Red Fife or triticale flour

2 cups (475 mL) vegetable stock, heated

2 Tbsp (30 mL) red miso (sold as "akamiso," it is darker in colour and stronger in flavour)

1 Tbsp (15 mL) birch, maple or agave syrup

1 Tbsp (15 mL) soy sauce

1 tsp (5 mL) toasted sesame oil

2 Tbsp (30 mL) nutritional yeast

Pinch of cayenne

2 Tbsp (30 mL) lowbush cranberries (optional)

1. Heat olive oil over medium heat in a small saucepan. Whisk in flour and cook for 3 to 4 minutes, until it just begins to brown. Pour in heated vegetable stock in a slow stream, whisking constantly. Whisk in remaining ingredients, including cranberries, if using. Reduce heat to medium low and simmer for 10 minutes to allow flavours to develop and sauce to thicken.

Baked Soybeans with Butternut Squash and Cranberries

MAKES 6 SERVINGS.

There's something particularly satisfying about the combination of nutty soybeans, soft, buttery squash and tart berries in this autumnal dish. Note that you'll need 2 cups (475 mL) of bean cooking water—save the cooking water when you make beans! *Vegan* IF COCONUT OIL IS USED

2 Tbsp (30 mL) olive oil

I medium onion, finely chopped

2 cloves garlic, minced

2 stalks celery, halved lengthwise and chopped

I tsp (5 mL) dried thyme

½ tsp (2.5 mL) cinnamon

Small butternut squash, chopped medium (about 4 cups/I L)

2 Tbsp (30 mL) tomato paste

6 Tbsp (90 mL) birch syrup, maple syrup or molasses

6 Tbsp (90 mL) apple cider vinegar

2 Tbsp (30 mL) soy sauce

2 Tbsp (30 mL) orange marmalade

4 cups (950 mL) cooked soybeans (for cooking instructions, see sidebar opposite)

I cup (250 mL) whole cranberries

2 cups (475 mL) bean cooking juice

2 Tbsp (30 mL) butter or coconut oil

1. Preheat oven to 325F (160C) and set the oven rack to the centre.

2. Heat oil in a 6-quart (6-L) ovenproof casserole dish (with a lid) over medium heat. Add onion and sauté until softened, 5 to 7 minutes. Add garlic and celery and sauté for another 3 to 4 minutes, until celery is softened, before stirring in thyme and cinnamon. Stir in squash and sauté for another 2 minutes.

3. Whisk together tomato paste, syrup, vinegar, soy sauce and marmalade. Pour over vegetables in the casserole dish. Stir in soybeans and cranberries. Add enough bean cooking juice to barely cover. Cover the casserole dish and bake for 90 minutes. Remove cover, stir in butter or coconut oil and return to the oven. Bake for another 30 minutes, or until most of the liquid is gone and what remains has thickened.

4. Serve in bowls accompanied by crusty bread and a green salad.

Above: In North America it's unusual to eat soybeans as whole foods, but they are very rewarding to cook whole: packed with nutrients, rich-tasting and high in protein. *Photo courtesy DarcyMaulsby/Thinkstock*

How to Cook Soybeans

Soak **dry soybeans** overnight. Use 3 cups (710 mL) water for every 1 cup (250 mL) soybeans; bring water to the boil, then add soybeans. Reduce heat, cover and simmer until al dente, about 90 minutes for homegrown soybeans, or at least 3 hours for store-bought. Drain and then continue with the recipe. Each cup (250 mL) raw soybeans will yield about 2 cups (475 mL) cooked.

TIP: Since soybeans take so long to cook, it's a good idea to make more than you need for a particular recipe. They'll keep in the fridge for up to a week, and you'll have them ready for adding to salads, soups or main course dishes.

Farro with Puttanesca Sauce

MAKES 4 SERVINGS.

Farro is the Italian term for different strains of wheat, in whole berry form—sometimes emmer, sometimes spelt or einkorn, and sometimes a combination of all three. Any one will do in this recipe—or go for rye berries. Start the grain cooking about 40 minutes before the sauce so everything will be ready at once. *Vegan* IF YOU SKIP THE PARMESAN

PUTTANESCA SAUCE

4 large cloves garlic, minced

¼ cup (60 mL) olive oil

28-oz (796-mL) can plum tomatoes

½ cup (120 mL) Kalamata olives, pitted and roughly chopped

1½ Tbsp (22 mL) capers, drained

¼ lemon, seeds removed, thinly sliced into triangles

1 tsp (5 mL) dried crushed red pepper

¼ cup (60 mL) packed, chopped parsley

FARRO

4 cups (950 mL) cooked whole farro (see sidebar on page 137 for cooking instructions)

1 Tbsp (15 mL) olive oil

1 clove garlic, minced

½ tsp (2.5 mL) freshly ground black pepper

1 cup (250 mL) grated Parmesan

1. Sauté garlic briefly in oil in a cast iron frying pan over medium heat. Add plum tomatoes, breaking them up with a fork. Stir in remaining sauce ingredients except parsley and simmer for 15 to 20 minutes, until flavours blend and sauce has thickened. Stir in parsley at the end.

2. Toss hot grain with olive oil, garlic and pepper and spoon into bowls. Ladle sauce over top, followed by a generous sprinkling of Parmesan cheese. Serve at once.

Triticale Pumpernickel-Style Sourdough Bread

MAKES TWO 9 × 5 × 2-INCH (22.5 × 13 × 5-CM) LOAVES.

A combination of triticale bread flour and whole triticale grain makes a dense, chewy sourdough bread with a sweet, nutty flavour. In this recipe, the triticale starter is "started off" with a sourdough starter made from all-purpose flour (see my previous book, *The Boreal Gourmet*, for more information about creating a starter from scratch; or you can order one online, or borrow from a friend). If you have a rye or whole wheat starter already going in your fridge, those will work too. As you continue to feed the triticale starter, with triticale flour, the percentage of other flour in the starter will gradually become negligible. This recipe usually takes between 17 and 22 hours from start to finish, so plan ahead!

TRITICALE STARTER

1 Tbsp (15 mL) sourdough rye, whole wheat or unbleached white flour starter

¼ cup (60 mL) plus 2 Tbsp (30 mL) triticale bread flour (or substitute dark rye flour, measure for measure), divided

¼ cup (60 mL) plus 2 Tbsp (30 mL) warm water, divided

SPONGE

2 cups (475 mL) triticale bread flour

2 cups (475mL) warm water

DOUGH

2 cups (475 mL) triticale bread flour

1 Tbsp (15 mL) salt

1 cup (250 mL) cooked triticale grain (see sidebar opposite for cooking instructions)

½ cup (120 mL) sunflower seeds

1. Whisk starter, 2 tablespoons (30 mL) triticale flour and 2 tablespoons (30 mL) warm water together in a large bowl. Cover with a plate and leave in a warm place for 6 to 8 hours, until doubled in size and small bubbles appear at the surface. It helps to use a clear bowl and mark the original level with magic marker on a piece of tape.

2. To the doubled starter, mix in additional ¼ cup (60 mL) triticale flour and ¼ cup (60 mL) warm water. Cover and mark the level. Once the starter has doubled again, after about 4 to 6 hours, measure out ½ cup (120 mL) of the mixture and store it in the fridge in an airtight container. You'll use this starter for future breads.

3. Make a sponge by adding the sponge ingredients to the bowl of remaining starter. Cover and mark the level. This time, the dough will be much more active, and could be ready in as little as 3 hours. When it's ready, the entire surface will be seamed and bubbling slowly and there will be small frothy bubbles forming.

4. With a wooden spoon, mix in dough ingredients. When they are thoroughly incorporated, tip dough out onto a work surface dusted with triticale flour. The dough will be both stiff and sticky, with a marked tendency to stick to the counter. A bread scraper will help to manipulate the dough. Knead for 2 to 3 minutes, sprinkling with additional flour as necessary to keep your hands from sticking.

5. Divide dough in half, shaping each half into a rough log. Transfer to two lightly greased 9 × 5-inch (22.5 × 13-cm) loaf pans, pressing dough lightly into the corners. Cover pans with a towel and let proof in a warm place for 3 to 4 hours, or until dough is nearly doubled in size, the surface is cracked and dough doesn't spring back when lightly pressed with a finger. The dough will be about 2 inches (5 cm) high.

6. While the dough proofs, preheat the oven to 450F (230C). Place a shallow pan of hot water on the bottom rack and set a rack in the middle of the oven.

7. Bake bread for 20 minutes. Carefully remove the pan of water, reduce heat to 400F (205C) and bake for another 10 minutes. Remove bread from pans and bake for an additional 5 minutes. The bread will not sound hollow when you tap it on the bottom, but will give a kind of muffled thunk.

8. Cool loaves on a wire rack. Resist cutting into the bread until it has thoroughly cooled. Store cooled loaves in brown paper bags. The loaves don't rise much and are quite dense; sliced, they make great appetizers or mid-afternoon snacks with cheese or almond butter.

 To cook whole triticale grain, add I part rinsed triticale to 3 parts boiling water. Bring to the boil again, reduce heat and simmer at medium-low heat for 50 to 60 minutes, until triticale is thoroughly cooked but still chewy. Pour off any excess cooking water. Serve right away or cool to room temperature before refrigerating for later use.

Yeasted Three-Grain Bread

MAKES 1 LOAF.

A highly flavoured, substantial loaf, great for toast and sandwiches.

2 ¼ tsp (10 mL) active dry yeast

1½ cups (350 mL) lukewarm water

2 Tbsp (30 mL) maple syrup

2 Tbsp (30 mL) birch syrup
or molasses

1 cup (250 mL) whole spelt flour

1 cup (250 mL) dark rye flour

1–2½ cups (250–600 mL) whole
wheat flour

1 Tbsp (15 mL) kosher salt

1 tsp (5 mL) fennel seeds

1. Dissolve yeast in the warm water. Once it has bloomed on the surface of the water, stir in syrups. In a separate bowl, whisk together the spelt and dark rye flours, 1 cup (250 mL) of the whole wheat flour, salt and fennel seeds. Add the yeast and syrup mixture to the dry ingredients, stirring with a wooden spoon until all the flour has been incorporated and the dough is a rough ball, neither dry nor sticky. If the dough is sticky, add more whole wheat flour.

2. With a scraper, transfer the dough to a lightly floured surface. Knead for 8 to 10 minutes, until dough is smooth. Form into a ball, coat lightly with olive oil, place in a clean bowl and cover with a tea towel. Set in a warm place out of direct sunlight to rise until doubled in size, about 2 hours.

3. Scrape dough onto a work surface dusted with flour and knead gently and briefly. Form into a ball once more. Place on a parchment-lined baking sheet, cover with a tea towel and let proof for 1 hour and 30 minutes to 2 hours, until the dough doesn't bounce back when you poke it with a finger. (The long proof is important to allow the dough to expand as much as possible.)

4. While the bread is proofing, preheat oven to 400F (205C), placing a pan of hot water on the bottom rack and setting a rack in the middle of the oven.

5. Bake the bread for 10 minutes. Remove the water (carefully), reduce heat to 350F (180C) and cook for another 45 to 50 minutes, until the bread sounds hollow when tapped on the bottom.

6. Cool on a rack. Resist cutting into the bread until it's thoroughly cooled.

Whole Wheat Chapatis with Toasted Flaxseeds

MAKES 12 CHAPATIS.

Why not make your own? There's really not much to it, except time, and they're so very good. Use them to scoop up Roasted Cauliflower, Barley and Hazelnut Pilaf (page 148).

1½ cups (350 mL) whole wheat flour

½ tsp (2.5 mL) salt

1 tsp (5 mL) flaxseeds, toasted

½ cup (120 mL) water

2 Tbsp (30 mL) melted butter or ghee

1. Whisk together flour, salt and seeds in a medium bowl. Stir in water until thoroughly mixed and a rough dough is formed.

2. Turn dough out onto a lightly floured work surface and knead until smooth, about 3 minutes. Cover with a damp cloth or plastic wrap and let rest for 10 minutes.

3. Divide dough into 12 equal pieces and roll each piece of dough into a ball. Cover dough balls with a damp cloth or plastic wrap and let rest for another 15 minutes.

4. Preheat a cast iron frying pan over medium heat.

5. Place one ball of dough on a lightly floured surface and pat down into a flat disc. Using a rolling pin, roll dough out to a 5-inch (13-cm) round. Cook chapati for 30 seconds per side, then brush on both sides with melted butter or ghee.

6. While each chapati cooks, begin rolling the next one (or, if you'd rather roll them all at once, stack the dough circles with a paper towel between each until ready to cook). After they're cooked, stack chapatis on a plate lined with a tea cloth, covered with a second tea cloth to keep them warm and soft.

7. As with pancakes, the last chapatis will cook more quickly than the first. Turn the heat to medium if the pan gets too hot. Serve warm chapatis at once.

Flaxseed Crackers

Adapted from Fäviken, by Magnus Nilsson.

MAKES ABOUT FORTY-FIVE 2-INCH (5-CM) CRACKERS.

These gossamer-thin, crunchy crackers are held together by potato starch and the gel-like coating released from flaxseeds when they are soaked in water. The crackers are see-through when you hold them up to the light, and make a great conversation piece as well as a delicious dipping cracker. They're also sturdy enough to support a piece of spreadable cheese like Brie or Camembert.

⅔ cup (160 mL) flaxseeds

¾ tsp (4 mL) salt

1 tsp (5 mL) anise, cumin or caraway seeds (optional)

1½ Tbsp (22 mL) potato starch

2 Tbsp (30 mL) cold water

1½ cups (350 mL) boiling water

1. Preheat oven to 325F (160C) and line three 9 × 13-inch (22.5 × 32-cm) baking sheets with parchment paper.

2. Dry-roast flaxseeds in a cast iron frying pan over medium heat for 5 minutes, or until they begin to crackle. Remove from heat and transfer seeds to a mixing bowl. Stir in salt and anise, cumin or caraway seeds, if using.

3. In a small bowl, dissolve potato starch in cold water. Gradually add in boiling water, whisking vigorously. Quickly whisk into the flaxseed mixture before the starch thickens and becomes unwieldy. Allow mixture to stand for 10 to 15 minutes, stirring occasionally, until thickened.

4. Divide flaxseed mixture evenly between the 3 baking sheets—about ⅔ cup (160 mL) per sheet. Spread mixture thinly and evenly over the parchment paper with an offset spatula. Ideally, there will be only one "layer" of seeds; otherwise the crackers will take an extra-long time to cook or will be chewy instead of crunchy.

5. Bake for 45 minutes, or until crackers are thoroughly dry to the touch, switching trays around halfway through to ensure even baking. (Note: The crackers shrink as they bake, causing the parchment paper to curl up. Fear not, this is normal.)

6. Remove from oven and cool in the pans on cooling trays. As crackers cool, it will be easy to peel them off the parchment paper. Break into serving-sized pieces and store in a tin. Crackers will keep indefinitely, but they're best consumed within a couple of weeks.

Red Fife and Buckwheat Flour Crackers

MAKES ABOUT FORTY-FIVE 2-INCH (5-CM) SQUARE OR ROUND CRACKERS.

The trick with these crackers is to roll them out as thinly as you can for maximum crispness.

I cup (250 mL) Red Fife wheat flour
¾ cup (180 mL) buckwheat flour
I tsp (5 mL) baking powder
I tsp (5 mL) cumin seeds, toasted
I tsp (5 mL) kosher salt

2 Tbsp (30 mL) flaxseeds
2 Tbsp (30 mL) pumpkin seeds
I Tbsp (15 mL) toasted
  pumpkin seed oil
¼ cup (60 mL) canola oil
6–8 Tbsp (90–120 mL) water

1. Preheat oven to 350F (180C) and set oven racks in the two middle positions.

2. Combine dry ingredients in the bowl of a food processor. Pulse until thoroughly mixed. Add oils and pulse until incorporated. Add water, 1 tablespoon (15 mL) at a time, until mixture holds together in one ball—if it's at all crumbly, add more water.

3. Divide dough into 3 parts. Lay out 3 baking sheet–sized pieces of parchment paper on a work surface. Using another sheet of paper over top, roll out the dough until it's ¹⁄₁₆-inch (0.16-cm) thick. (The thinner the dough, the crunchier the cracker.)

4. With a sharp knife, cut dough into even squares (without cutting the paper), about 2 inches (5 cm) square. Separate squares slightly from each other before baking. Alternatively, use a 2-inch (5-cm) round cookie cutter, and keep rolling and cutting until all the dough is used up.

5. Slide the parchment paper onto baking sheets. Bake for 20 minutes, until crisp and lightly browned, switching the baking sheets around halfway through. Cool on a rack and store in a tin. Will keep for up to 1 week.

Almond Cashew Oat Bars

This energy-giving treat is a proven favourite with campers and trekkers.

1½ cups (350 mL) rolled oats
¾ cup (180 mL) raw cashews
1 cup (250 mL) packed pitted dates
½ tsp (2.5 mL) kosher salt
¼ cup (60 mL) almond butter

3.5 oz (100 gr) dark chocolate, at least 70 percent cocoa, broken into pieces
¼ cup (60 mL) birch syrup or honey
2 Tbsp (30 mL) milled flaxseeds or shredded, unsweetened coconut

1. Preheat oven to 350F (180C).

2. Toast oats and cashews on 2 baking sheets for 10 minutes. Remove from oven and cool to room temperature. Finely chop cashews.

3. Grind dates in a food processor until they form into a compact ball. Transfer to a bowl and combine with the oats, chopped cashews and salt, using a fork or your fingers to break up the dates and blend ingredients evenly.

4. Melt almond butter, chocolate and birch syrup in a small saucepan over medium heat, stirring occasionally. Pour over the dry ingredients, blending thoroughly with a wooden spoon.

5. Line an 8-inch (20-cm) square baking pan with plastic wrap. Spoon mixture into the pan. Place a second piece of plastic wrap overtop and press mixture evenly into the pan, levelling the top as much as possible.

6. Place the mixture, covered, in the freezer to set for 15 minutes. Tip out onto a work surface and unwrap. Slice into 16 squares. Pour flaxseeds or coconut onto a plate and coat each square thoroughly. Pack into small resealable bags and freeze until ready to eat. Squares will keep, unrefrigerated, for 3 to 4 weeks.

Pumpkin Seed Butter Cookies

Adapted from The Joy of Cooking's peanut butter cookie recipe.

MAKES ABOUT 35 COOKIES.

Here's a peanut butter cookie for those who can't eat peanuts, and a real treat for the pumpkin seed lovers amongst us.

½ cup (120 mL) butter, softened

½ cup (120 mL), packed organic brown sugar

½ cup (120 mL) organic cane sugar

1 large egg

1 cup (250 mL) pumpkin seed butter

½ tsp (2.5 mL) salt

½ tsp (2.5 mL) baking soda

½ tsp (2.5 mL) vanilla

1¼–1½ cups (300–350 mL) whole spelt flour

½ cup (120 mL) pumpkin seeds, roughly chopped

1. Preheat oven to 375F (190C) and line 3 baking sheets with parchment.

2. Beat butter until light and fluffy. Gradually beat in sugars, followed by the egg, and beat thoroughly to combine. Beat in pumpkin seed butter, and when fully incorporated, beat in salt, baking soda and vanilla. Stir in flour (using larger amount if dough is too moist), followed by pumpkin seeds.

3. Scoop 1-tablespoon (15-mL) balls of dough onto prepared baking sheets, about 12 per sheet, leaving room to spread in between. Press the dough balls flat with the tines of a fork.

4. Bake for 10 to 12 minutes, switching the trays around halfway through so they cook evenly. Cool on baking sheets for 5 minutes, then transfer to a wire rack to cool completely. Store in a tin in a cool dark cupboard and eat within a couple of days, or freeze in small batches for up to three months.

Rhubarb Coconut Cookies

MAKES 45 TO 55 COOKIES.

If you make a lot of rhubarb syrup, you end up with a lot of rhubarb purée! Happily the purée is a great addition to baked goods, from breads to muffins to cookies. Here powdered ginger works with the rhubarb to add tang, while currants and coconut provide sweetness and texture.

½ cup (120 mL) butter, softened (or substitute softened coconut oil)

1 cup (250 mL) plus 2 Tbsp (30 mL) coconut sugar, divided

1 egg (or substitute 1 vegan flax egg; see sidebar on page 102)

1 cup (250 mL) rhubarb purée (about 2 cups/475 mL chopped rhubarb; see Morning Glory Quinoa Muffins, page 107, for cooking instructions)

1 Tbsp (15 mL) grated orange zest (1 large orange)

2 cups (475 mL) triticale flour

1½ tsp (7.5 mL) baking powder

½ tsp (2.5 mL) baking soda

1 tsp (5 mL) ground ginger

1 cup (250 mL) shredded, unsweetened coconut

½ cup (120 mL) flaxseeds

1 cup (250 mL) dried currants

1. Preheat oven to 350F (180C) and line 3 baking sheets with parchment paper.

2. In a large bowl, cream butter until soft and fluffy. Sift 1 cup (250 mL) coconut sugar overtop and stir until thoroughly combined. Whisk in egg, followed by rhubarb and orange zest.

3. In a separate bowl, whisk together flour, baking powder, baking soda and ginger. Stir remaining ingredients into the flour mixture, breaking up currants with your fingers if necessary. Stir dry ingredients into wet, making sure they're thoroughly incorporated.

4. For softer cookies, scoop or drop tablespoonsful (15 mL) of dough onto the paper, leaving about 1 inch (2.5 cm) between them. (The cookies don't spread much.) For chewier cookies, flatten dough with a fork or the palm of your hand, dusted lightly with flour.

5. Sift remaining 2 tablespoons (30 mL) of sugar over top of the cookies. Bake for 15 to 18 minutes, or until tops are lightly browned.

6. Cool on a rack. Store in a tin in a cool dark cupboard and eat within a week, or freeze in small batches for up to 3 months.

Alegria—Mexican Popped Amaranth Squares

MAKES SIXTEEN 2½-INCH (6.5-CM) SQUARES.

Alegria means "joy" in Spanish, and successfully making these traditional Mexican bars is certainly a joyful experience. So is eating them. The popped amaranth is light and crunchy, with a bit of smokiness from the high heat needed to pop it. This is definitely a trial-and-error recipe, so if at first you don't succeed ... you know the rest.

½ cup (120 mL) raw amaranth seeds

¼ cup (60 mL) raw, unsalted pumpkin seeds

¼ cup (60 mL) dried currants or cranberries

1 cup (250 mL) maple syrup

1. Popping amaranth seeds without burning them can be tricky, and it might take a couple of tries to get it right. For best results use a small, lidded frying pan that can take high heat. The lid is crucial—like popping corn, popping amaranth flies everywhere.

2. Have the amaranth seeds ready in a bowl beside the frying pan, along with a 1-tablespoon (15-mL) measure, a clean bowl and a wooden spoon. And oven mitts—the pan will get hot.

3. Place the pan over medium-high heat until smoking hot. Pour no more than 1 tablespoon (15 mL) of seeds into the pan and cover immediately. The seeds should start to pop right away. Agitate the pan over the burner, as you would with popcorn, for about 10 to 15 seconds, or until the seeds are popping rapidly. Remove the pan from the heat and shake a few times to pop any stragglers. Transfer the popped seeds to the clean bowl, scraping them out of the pan with the spoon. (Any seeds left behind are liable to burn, flavouring the whole batch.) Allow the pan to heat up for a few seconds between batches. Repeat until all the seeds have popped. You should have 2 cups (475 mL).

Continued on page 176

ALEGRIA—MEXICAN POPPED AMARANTH SQUARES CONTINUED

4. Remove the pan from heat and allow to cool briefly, then dry-roast pumpkin seeds over medium heat until they begin to crackle and pop, about 3 to 4 minutes. Remove from heat and add to the amaranth seeds. Stir in dried fruit.

5. In a small saucepan, bring maple syrup to a boil over medium-high heat, then turn heat to medium and boil until syrup is reduced by half, about 5 to 7 minutes. Immediately stir into amaranth mixture, making sure to mix thoroughly.

6. Transfer to a parchment-lined 9-inch (22.5-cm) square baking pan. Lay another piece of parchment overtop and press mixture firmly into the pan.

7. Once cool, remove the *alegria* from the pan by picking up the ends of the parchment paper. Place the squares on a cutting board, remove paper and cut into 16 squares.

Dan Jason photo

Quinoa Brownies

MAKES SIXTEEN 2-INCH (5-CM) SQUARES.

Fudge-like, rich, delicious.

¾ cup (180 mL) organic cane sugar
½ cup (120 mL) cocoa powder
I tsp (5 mL) baking powder
¼ tsp (I mL) salt
½ cup (120 mL) dark chocolate chips
½ cup (120 mL) chopped walnuts

1½ cups (350 mL) cooked red or black quinoa (for cooking instructions, see How to Enjoy Quinoa Seed, page 64)
2 large eggs
2 Tbsp (30 mL) coconut oil, melted
¼ cup (60 mL) milk
I tsp (5 mL) vanilla

1. Preheat oven to 350F (180C) and oil an 8-inch (20-cm) square baking pan

2. Whisk dry ingredients together, stirring in chocolate chips and walnuts at the end.

3. Combine cooked quinoa and wet ingredients in the bowl of a food processor and blend until smooth, about 1 minute. Add quinoa mixture to dry ingredients and stir until just combined.

4. Pour batter into baking pan, smoothing the top. Bake for 30 to 35 minutes, or until the middle feels firm to the touch. (The toothpick test doesn't work for these brownies, because you actually want them to be slightly fudgy.) Cool on a rack. Serve right from the pan with some raspberry ice cream on the side.

Chocolate Soybean Turinois

MAKES 1 LOAF, ENOUGH FOR 12-16 SERVINGS.

Here is a rich, deeply chocolaty dessert for a special occasion. This version of the classic French *Turinois* is adapted from Nigella Lawson's *Feast,* substituting cooked, ground Cha Kura Kake soybeans ounce per ounce for chestnut purée.

17.5 oz (500 gr) whole cooked pale, organic soybeans (about 3 cups/710 mL; for cooking instructions, see sidebar on page 157)

3 Tbsp (45 mL) dark rum

6 oz (160 gr) unsalted butter, softened (about ¾ cup/180 mL)

3 Tbsp (45 mL) honey

¼ cup (60 mL) cocoa powder

1 tsp (5 mL) salt

10.5 oz (300 gr) 70 percent chocolate

Cocoa, for dusting

1. Purée soybeans and rum in the bowl of a food processor until smooth (there may be small flecks of soybean skin still visible). Add softened butter, honey, cocoa powder and salt to the mixture and purée again.

2. Melt chocolate in the top of a double boiler over simmering water. Remove from heat, allow to cool slightly, and then add to soybean mixture. Purée until completely blended.

3. Line a 9 × 5-inch (22.5 × 13-cm) loaf pan with plastic wrap, large enough to overhang the ends by several inches. Spoon the chocolate-soybean mixture into the pan, pressing it into the ends and sides of the pan. Smooth the top with an offset spatula. Fold the plastic overtop so the Turinois is completely covered. Refrigerate for several hours or overnight.

4. To serve, unwrap Turinois and place on a work surface dusted with cocoa. Cut into ½-inch (1.25-cm) slices. Serve with crème fraîche on the side, garnished with a couple of fresh berries.

TIP: When **puréeing cooked soybeans,** you'll need to add 2 or 3 Tbsp (30–45 mL) of liquid to achieve a smooth texture. When substituting soybeans for chestnut purée in other recipes, purée part of the rum or other liquid in the recipe with the soybeans.

Individual Strawberry Shortcakes with Flaky Whole Grain Biscuits

MAKES 12 INDIVIDUAL SHORTCAKES.

Over the years I've learned strawberry shortcake is best when all the components are made the day the dessert is served—ideally, in the late afternoon before dinner. Biscuits are best fresh, strawberries too—but whipped cream, Drambuie and maple syrup will keep in the fridge for a few hours, so you can do that step in advance to save time later.

STRAWBERRIES

1½ lbs (620 gr) strawberries, washed, hulled and sliced (about 6 cups/1.4 L)

¼ cup (60 mL) organic cane sugar

BISCUITS

1½ cups (350 mL) whole wheat cake flour

4 tsp (20 mL) baking powder

½ tsp (2.5 mL) salt

I Tbsp (15 mL) organic cane sugar

½ cup (120 mL) cold butter, diced

I cup (250 mL) flaked quinoa

½ cup (120 mL) plain yogurt (plus 2 Tbsp/30 mL if needed)

WHIPPED CREAM

I cup (250 mL) 35 percent cream

I Tbsp (15 mL) maple syrup

I Tbsp (15 mL) Drambuie or whisky

1. Preheat oven to 450F (230C) and set a rack in the middle of the oven.

2. Prepare the strawberries a few hours before serving. The sugar will draw liquid out of the strawberries to make a light syrup. Combine the ingredients together in a medium bowl, cover and refrigerate until ready to assemble.

3. To make biscuits, combine flour, baking powder, salt and sugar in the bowl of a food processor. Pulse once or twice to mix. Add butter pieces and pulse until the mixture resembles coarse crumbs with a few pea-sized pieces of butter remaining.

Continued on page 182

4. Transfer mixture to a bowl and stir in flaked quinoa. Add ½ cup (120 mL) yogurt and mix with a fork. If mixture appears too dry and crumbly, add the remaining 2 tablespoons (30 mL) yogurt—dough will still be crumbly but a piece pinched between the fingers should hold together.

5. Tip dough onto a lightly floured surface and, pressing lightly with your hands, form into a circle about 9 inches (22.5 cm) in diameter and ¾ inch (2 cm) high. Cut into rounds with a 2½-inch (6.5-cm) cookie cutter dipped in flour. Pat remaining dough into a circle and cut again until all the dough is used up and you have 12 rounds—you may need to form the last biscuit with your hands.

6. Bake for 10 to 12 minutes, until biscuit tops are golden brown. Cool on a rack to room temperature before slicing to make strawberry shortcakes.

7. When ready to assemble, whip cream until soft peaks form. Add the maple syrup and Drambuie, still whipping, until stiff peaks form. Refrigerate until ready to use if not assembling right away.

8. To assemble, slice biscuits in half. Spoon strawberries over the bottom half, followed by a spoonful of syrup and a generous dollop of whipped cream. Place the other biscuit half over top and finish with spoonful of cream and a couple of strawberries. Serve at once.

Barley, Almond and Anise Pudding

Adapted from Dan's recipe, this custardy pudding is fabulous with whipped cream and toasted slivered almonds.

MAKES 6 TO 8 SERVINGS.

2 cups (475 mL) water
⅔ cup (160 mL) raw barley
1⅓ cups (330 mL) milk
2 eggs, lightly beaten
1 Tbsp (15 mL) butter, melted
1 tsp (5 mL) pure almond extract
¼ cup (60 mL) organic brown sugar
¼ tsp (1 mL) salt

1 tsp (5 mL) anise seeds
½ cup (120 mL) chopped
   dried apricots

GARNISH

½ cup (120 mL) 35 percent cream
2 Tbsp (30 mL) toasted
   slivered almonds

1. Boil water. Rinse the barley, then add to boiling water, cover, bring to a boil again, reduce heat and simmer until soft but still chewy, about 40 to 50 minutes, checking after 40 minutes. Drain off excess water.

2. Preheat oven to 325F (160C) and set a rack in the middle of the oven. Grease an 8-inch (20-cm) square baking pan.

3. Beat together the milk, eggs, butter, almond extract, sugar, salt and anise seeds. Stir in barley and apricots.

4. Pour into prepared baking pan and set inside a larger baking pan. Fill larger pan with hot water to within ¾ inch (2 cm) of the top of the custard pan. Bake for about 55 minutes, then remove the custard pan from the water and bake for another 5 minutes. When the pudding is done, a knife inserted in the centre should come out clean.

5. Serve warm or cold. To serve, whip the cream until soft peaks form. Top each serving with a spoonful of cream and a sprinkling of almonds.

Carrot, Banana and Triticale Loaf

MAKES 1 LOAF.

A rich, moist, dense bread that keeps well, great for canoe trips and hikes or for an afternoon pick-me-up with a cup of coffee or tea. *Vegan* IF YOU USE FLAX EGGS

⅓ cup (80 mL) coconut oil, melted

2 eggs (or substitute 2 flax eggs; see sidebar on page 102)

1 cup (250 mL) mashed bananas (2–3 bananas)

1 cup (250 mL) grated carrots (1 large carrot)

2 cups (475 mL) triticale pastry flour (or substitute an equal amount of whole spelt flour, or a mixture of 1½ cups/350 mL whole wheat and ½ cup/120mL rye flour)

1 cup (250 mL) coconut sugar

½ tsp (2.5 mL) salt

1 tsp (5 mL) ground cardamom

½ tsp (2.5 mL) ground ginger

1½ tsp (7.5 mL) baking soda

½ cup (120 mL) chopped Mission figs

½ cup (120 mL) chopped pecans

1. Preheat oven to 350F (180C), place rack in the middle of the oven and oil a 9 × 5-inch (22.5 × 13-cm) loaf pan.

2. In a medium bowl, whisk together coconut oil and eggs until foamy. Beat in bananas and carrots.

3. In a separate bowl, whisk together dry ingredients, adding figs and pecans last.

4. Stir dry ingredients into wet just until combined. Spoon into loaf pan. Bake for 1 hour, or until a toothpick inserted in the middle of the loaf comes out clean. Cool in the pan for 20 minutes, then remove from the pan and cool to room temperature. Resist cutting into the bread before it has cooled to avoid crumbly slices. Will keep, wrapped in plastic and stored in a tin, for up to 3 weeks.

Soybean "Chestnut" Torte

Inspired by Caroline Wright's Chestnut-Marsala Torte.

MAKES 8 TO 12 SERVINGS.

This moist torte is a wonderful weeknight dessert, yet it is elegant enough to attend your next dinner party. If you can't find Cha Kura Kake soybeans, use any pale, organic variety.

1½ cups (350 mL) cooked soybeans (for cooking instructions, see sidebar on page 157)

1 tsp (5 mL) liquid honey

¼ cup (60 mL) 3.5 percent milk

1 cup (250 mL) unsalted butter, softened

1 cup (250 mL) organic cane sugar

2 large eggs

¼ cup (60 mL) sherry, Marsala or Madeira

1 cup (250 mL) whole spelt flour

1 cup (250 mL) whole wheat flour

2 tsp (10 mL) baking powder

¼ tsp (1 mL) freshly grated nutmeg

1 cup (250 mL) chopped dried apricots

Confectioner's sugar, for dusting

1. Preheat oven to 350F (180C) and set a rack in the middle of the oven. Butter a 9-inch (22.5-cm) round pan with a removable bottom.

2. Purée cooked soybeans with honey and milk until the mixture is the texture of coarse pâté.

3. In a separate bowl, beat butter until soft and fluffy. Gradually beat in sugar. Beat in eggs, one at a time, followed by the sherry and the soybean purée.

4. Sift together flours, baking powder and nutmeg in a small bowl. Add chopped apricots, tossing with your fingers to coat the pieces with flour and distribute evenly.

5. Stir dry ingredients into wet ingredients just until mixed. Spoon into pan and smooth the top of the cake with the back of a spoon or an offset spatula.

6. Bake for 55 to 60 minutes, or until the cake pulls away from the sides of the pan. Cool for 10 minutes in the pan, then remove rim and cool completely on a wire rack. Sprinkle with confectioner's sugar just before serving.

ENDNOTES

1   News.com.au: *Ancient Grains* (http://www.news.com.au/lifestyle/food/ancient
    -grains-why-you-should-eat-these-six-superfoods-eaten-by-the-aztec/news-story
    /d9972262icf9c7ef22d378be8e8bcc4e)

2   *Science Daily* (https://www.sciencedaily.com/releases/2009/12/091217141312.htm)

3   Fieldstone Organics (http://fieldstoneorganics.ca/organic-benefits/ancient-grains.php)

4   David Suzuki Foundation (http://www.davidsuzuki.org/what-you-can-do/food-and-our-planet
    /food-and-climate-change/)

5   Salt Spring Seeds is online at: https://www.saltspringseeds.com/

6   Wild Garden Seed: *Amaranthus spp.* Seeds per ounce: 30,000 (https://www.wildgardenseed.com
    /index.php?cPath=26&osCsid=0afab8444b0d6d3b2c60a1e4144ee1ec)

7   Random House, Inc., September 1991

8   *National Geographic* (http://news.nationalgeographic.com
    /news/2013/08/130812-amaranth-oaxaca-mexico-obesity-puente-food/)

9   ThoughtCo: "Amaranth has been a staple in Mesoamerica for thousands of years, first collected
    as a wild food, and then domesticated at least as early as 4000 BC." (https://www.thoughtco.com
    /amaranth-origin-169487)

10 *Lost Crops of the Incas* (https://www.nap.edu/read/1398/chapter/16#146)

11 The World's Healthiest Foods (http://whfoods.org/genpage.php?tname=dailytip&dbid=231)

12 The Amaranth Institute: "Table 2: Nutritional Information for Amaranth and Similar Leaves"
    (http://amaranthinstitute.org/sites/default/files/docs/NutritionalInformationforAmaranth.pdf)

13 Inkanat (http://www.inkanat.com/en/arti.asp?ref=amaranth-grain)

14 SELF Nutrition Data (http://nutritiondata.self.com/facts/cereal-grains-and-pasta/5676/2)

15 Food Facts by Mercola (http://foodfacts.mercola.com/amaranth.html)

16 Grains & Legumes Nutrition Council (http://www.glnc.org.au/grains-2/types-of-grains/amaranth/)

17 The World's Healthiest Foods (http://whfoods.org/genpage.php?tname=dailytip&dbid=231)

18 SELF Nutrition Data (http://nutritiondata.self.com/facts/cereal-grains-and-pasta/5676/2)

19 Mayo Clinic: Gluten-free Diet (http://www.mayoclinic.org/healthy-lifestyle
    /nutrition-and-healthy-eating/in-depth/gluten-free-diet/art-20048530)

20 United States Department of Agriculture (USDA) (https://portal.nifa.usda.gov/web
    /crisprojectpages/0206915-herbicide-resistance-in-weedy-amaranthus-species.html)

21 Grist (http://grist.org/food/this-weed-is-taking-over-the-planet-on-the-up-side-its-delicious/)

22 Seed Savers Exchange is online at http://www.seedsavers.org/

23 USC Canada (http://usc-canada.org/what-we-do/seeds-of-survival/)

24 SELF Nutrition Data (http://nutritiondata.self.com/facts/cereal-grains-and-pasta/5678/2)

25 Dr. Axe: Food is Medicine (https://draxe.com/barley-nutrition/)

26 Health Canada (http://www.hc-sc.gc.ca/fn-an/label-etiquet/claims-reclam/assess-evalu
    /barley-orge-eng.php)

27 The World's Healthiest Foods (http://www.whfoods.com/genpage.php?tname=foodspice&dbid=127)

28 The World's Healthiest Foods (http://www.whfoods.com/genpage.php?tname=foodspice&dbid=11)

29 The Biology Project, Department of Biochemistry and Molecular Biophysics, University of Arizona: The
    Chemistry of Amino Acids (http://www.biology.arizona.edu/biochemistry/problem_sets
    /aa/aa.html)

30 SELF Nutrition Data (http://nutritiondata.self.com/facts/cereal-grains-and-pasta/5683/2)

31 Berkeley Wellness, University of California (http://www.berkeleywellness.com/healthy-eating/food
    /article/buckwheat-low-gluten-high-nutrients)

32 Authority Nutrition (https://authoritynutrition.com/foods/buckwheat/#Nutrition_facts)

33 ResearchGate: *Rutin in buckwheat—Protection of plants and its importance for the production of functional food*
    (https://www.researchgate.net/publication/255602730_Rutin_in_buckwheat_-
    _Protection_of_plants_and_its_importance_for_the_production_of_functional_food)

34 Mayo Clinic: Gluten-free Diet (http://www.mayoclinic.org/healthy-lifestyle
    /nutrition-and-healthy-eating/in-depth/gluten-free-diet/art-20048530)

35 Authority Nutrition (https://authoritynutrition.com/foods/buckwheat/#Nutrition_facts)

36 The World's Healthiest Foods (http://www.healwithfood.org/gallstones/foods.php)

37 The World's Healthiest Foods (http://www.whfoods.com/genpage.php?tname=foodspice&dbid=11)

38 SELF Nutrition Data (http://nutritiondata.self.com/facts/nut-and-seed-products/3163/2)

39 *Medical News Today: Flaxseed* (http://www.medicalnewstoday.com/articles/263405.php)

40 Dr. Axe: Food is Medicine (https://draxe.com/10-flax-seed-benefits-nutrition-facts/)

41 Ibid.

42 Flax Council: "Flax is one of the richest sources of plant lignans, being very rich in the lignan secoisolariciresinol
    diglucoside. Flax contains other lignans as well—namely, matairesinol, pinoresinol, lariciresinol, isolariciresinol
    and secoisolariciresinol." (http://flaxcouncil.ca/wp-content/uploads/2015/03/FlxPrmr_4ed_Chpt4.pdf)

43 Natural News: *Flaxseeds are packed with fatty acids, lignans and minerals* (http://www.naturalnews
    .com/045572_flaxseeds_lignans_fatty_acids.html)

44 Dr. Axe: Food is Medicine (https://draxe.com/10-flax-seed-benefits-nutrition-facts/)

45 Oregon State University Linus Pauling Institute Micronutrient Information Center (http://lpi
    .oregonstate.edu/mic/dietary-factors/phytochemicals/lignans#food-sources)

46 The World's Healthiest Foods (http://www.whfoods.com/genpage.php?tname=foodspice&dbid=81)

47 Flax Council (http://flaxcouncil.ca/wp-content/uploads/2015/03/FlxPrmr_4ed_Chpt6.pdf)

48 *Silver Bulletin e-News Magazine* (http://silverbulletin.utopiasilver.com
    /flax-hull-lignans-may-the-the-most-promising-anti-cancer-breakthrough/)

49 WebMD: *The Benefits of Flaxseed* (http://www.webmd.com/diet/features/benefits-of-flaxseed#1)

50 Flax Council (http://flaxcouncil.ca/wp-content/uploads/2015/03/FlxPrmr_4ed_Chpt5.pdf)

51 HealthyFlax.org (https://healthyflax.org/news/flaxfaq-are-there-any-permitted-health
    -claims-for-flaxseed)

52 The World's Healthiest Foods (http://www.whfoods.com/genpage.php?tname=foodspice&dbid=81)

53 Dietitians of Canada (http://www.dietitians.ca/Your-Health/Nutrition-A-Z/Fibre/Food-Sources-of
    -Fibre.aspx)

54 Mayo Clinic (http://www.mayoclinic.org/healthy-lifestyle/nutrition-and-healthy-eating/in-depth
    /gluten-free-diet/art-20048530)

55 The World's Healthiest Foods (http://www.whfoods.org/genpage.php?tname=foodspice&dbid=81)

56 OMICS International: *Pumpkin seed oil* (http://research.omicsgroup.org/index.php
    /Pumpkin_seed_oil)

57 Dr. Axe: Food is Medicine (https://draxe.com/pumpkin-seed-oil/)

58 Real Raw Food (http://realrawfood.com/pumpkinseeds-styrian-health-benefits-and
    -nutritional-info)

59   ResearchGate: *Seeds and oil of the Styrian oil pumpkin: Components and biological activities* (http://www.styriangold.ca/wp-content/uploads/2016/02/Seeds-and-oil-of-the-Styrian-oil-pumpkin_ Components-and-biological-activities.pdf) and US National Library of Medicine National Institutes of Health: *Effects of pumpkin seed oil and saw palmetto in Korean men with symptomatic benign prostatic hyperplasia* (https://www.ncbi.nlm.nih.gov/pmc/articles/PMC2809240/)

60   *Health Benefits Times: Health Benefits of Pumpkin Seed Oil* (https://www.healthbenefitstimes.com /health-benefits-pumpkin-seed-oil/)

61   Smart Eaters (http://www.smarteaters.org/news-and-views/news-articles/news-pumpkin-seed-hypertension .html)

62   GreenMedInfo (http://www.greenmedinfo.com/blog/remarkable-healing-properties-pumpkin-seed)

63   Superfood Profiles: *Pumpkin Seeds for Parasites and Intestinal Worms* (http://superfoodprofiles.com /pumpkin-seeds-parasites-intestinal-worms)

64   Cucurbit Genetics Cooperative Crop Genetics Cooperatives: *The Health Value of Styrian Pumpkin Seed Oil— Science and Fiction* (http://cuke.hort.ncsu.edu/cgc/cgc23/cgc23-41.html)

65   Dr. Axe: Food is Medicine (https://draxe.com/pumpkin-seed-oil/)

66   The World's Healthiest Foods (http://www.whfoods.com/genpage.php?tname=foodspice&dbid=82)

67   Food Facts by Mercola (http://articles.mercola.com/sites/articles/archive/2013/09/30 /pumpkin-seed-benefits.aspx)

68   More on this book at this website: http://patriciaandcarolyn.com /qunioa-365-the-everyday-superfood/

69   The National Academies Press: Quinoa (https://www.nap.edu/read/1398/chapter/17#149)

70   Natural News (http://www.naturalnews.com/046879_quinoa_complete_protein_gluten_free.html)

71   Quinoa: 2013 International Year, Food and Agriculture Organization of the United Nations (http://www.fao.org/quinoa-2013/what-is-quinoa/nutritional-value/en/)

72   SELF Nutrition Data (http://nutritiondata.self.com/facts/cereal-grains-and-pasta/10352/2)

73   Quinoa: 2013 International Year, Food and Agriculture Organization of the United Nations (http://www.fao.org/quinoa-2013/what-is-quinoa/nutritional-value/en/)

74   Mayo Clinic (http://www.mayoclinic.org/healthy-lifestyle/nutrition-and-healthy-eating/in-depth /gluten-free-diet/art-20048530)

75   Grains & Legumes Nutrition Council (http://www.glnc.org.au/grains-2/types-of-grains/quinoa/)

76   The World's Healthiest Foods (http://www.whfoods.com/genpage.php?tname=foodspice&dbid=142)

77   AminoAcidStudies.org (http://aminoacidstudies.org/l-histidine/)

78   The World's Healthiest Foods (http://www.whfoods.com/genpage.php?tname=foodspice&dbid=142)

79   US National Library of Medicine National Institutes of Health (https://www.ncbi.nlm.nih.gov /pubmed/19735168)

80   Natural News (http://www.naturalnews.com/046879_quinoa_complete_protein_gluten_free.html)

81   The World's Healthiest Foods (http://www.whfoods.com/genpage.php?tname=foodspice&dbid=142)

82   The Science of Eating (http://thescienceofeating.com/2016/10/31/saponins-lower-cholesterol-boost -immune-system-fight-cancer-many-other-benefits-heres-how-to-get-them/)

83   The World's Healthiest Foods (http://www.whfoods.com/genpage.php?tname=foodspice&dbid=79)

84   Healthy Living (http://healthyliving.azcentral.com/legumes-amino-acids-3708.html)

85   SoyConnection By the United Soybean Board (http://www.soyconnection.com/soy-foods /nutritional-composition)

86   Dietitians of Canada (http://www.dietitians.ca/Your-Health/Nutrition-A-Z/Soy/Health-Benefits -of-Soy.aspx)

87   Cowspiracy: The Sustainability Secret (http://www.cowspiracy.com/facts/)

88   https://link.springer.com/article/10.1007%2Fs10584-014-1169-1/fulltext.html

89   Organic Consumers Association (https://www.organicconsumers.org/campaigns/millions-against-monsanto)

90   Natural Society: *Top 10 Companies Killing the Natural World With Pesticides—Also The Biggest Seed Producers* (http://naturalsociety.com/top-6-companies-killing-natural-world-pesticides-also-bigg- est-seed-producers/)

91 GMO Compass (http://greenearthsystems.com.au/commodities/soy/)

    Industry Week: GMO Corn, Soybeans Dominate US Market: (https://www.ers.usda.gov/data-products /adoption-of-genetically-engineered-crops-in-the-us/recent-trends-in-ge-adoption.aspx)

92 *GMO Myths and Truths, 2nd edition* (http://earthopensource.org/wp-content/uploads/2014/11 /GMO-Myths-and-Truths-edition2.pdf)

93 "Engineered Food and Your Health: The Nutritional Status of GMOs," a public lecture by Dr. Thierry Vrain at Trent University in Peterborough, ON, November 16, 2014.

94 Center for Food Safety (http://www.centerforfoodsafety.org/files/glyphosate-faq_64013.pdf)

95 Canadian Biotechnology Action Network (CBAN) GMO Inquiry 2015 (http://gmoinquiry.ca/wp -content/uploads/2015/03/where-in-the-world-gm-crops-foods.pdf)

96 Annapolis Seeds is online at: http://www.annapolisseeds.com/

97 Global News: *Canada's potential to feed the world focus of Breadbasket Summit* (http://globalnews .ca/news/650987/canadas-potential-to-feed-the-world-focus-of-breadbasket-summit/)

98 Penguin, June 2016 (http://www.stephenyafa.com/)

99 Harvard T.H. Chan School of Public Health: *More whole grains linked with lower mortality* (https://www.hsph.harvard.edu/news/press-releases/more-whole-grains-linked-with -lower-mortality-risk/)

100 Harvard T.H. Chan School of Public Health: *Eating more whole grains linked with lower mortality rates* (https:// www.hsph.harvard.edu/news/press-releases/whole-grains-lower-mortality-rates/)

101 SELF Nutrition Data (http://nutritiondata.self.com/facts/cereal-grains-and-pasta/5744/2)

102 Grains & Legumes Nutrition Council (http://www.glnc.org.au/grains-2/types-of-grains/wheat/) and Authority Nutrition: *Wheat 101: Nutrition Facts and Health Effects* (https://authoritynutrition.com/foods/wheat/)

103 American Institute for Cancer Research (http://www.aicr.org/foods-that-fight-cancer/whole -grains.html)

104 The World's Healthiest Foods (http://www.whfoods.com/genpage.php?tname=foodspice&dbid=66)

105 The Whole Grain Connection (http://wholegrainconnection.org/)

106 Historica Canada: *Red Fife Wheat* (http://www.thecanadianencyclopedia.com/en/article /red-fife-wheat/)

107 Historica Canada: *Marquis Wheat* (http://www.thecanadianencyclopedia.ca/en/article /marquis-wheat/)

108 Kamut Brand Khorasan Wheat: *The Story* (http://www.kamut.com/en/discover/the-story)

109 The World's Healthiest Foods (http://www.whfoods.com/genpage.php?tname=foodspice&dbid=65)

110 The World's Healthiest Foods (http://www.whfoods.com/genpage.php?tname=foodspice&dbid=54)

111 SELF Nutrition Data (http://nutritiondata.self.com/facts/cereal-grains-and-pasta/5734/2)

112 For more on growing each grain or seed, an online source of information is https://sproutpeople .org/growing-sprouts/

113 The Hippocrates Institute (http://hippocratesinst.org/benefits-of-wheatgrass-2)

114 An online source of information on how to consume wheatgrass juice for health is Happy Juicer. (http://www. happyjuicer.com/juicing-information/juicing-for-health.aspx)

115 Dr. Mercola: Wheatgrass is "a detoxifying herb and should not be consumed every day for long periods of time" (http://articles.mercola.com/sites/articles/archive/2013/05/20/wheatgrass.aspx)

116 GlutenFreeLiving (https://www.glutenfreeliving.com/gluten-free-foods/gluten-free-nutrition /gluten-questions-and-answers/wheat-grass/)

INDEX

GARDENING INDEX

RECIPE INDEX

Page numbers in **bold** refer to photos

Left: Dan Jason. *Photo courtesy Derek Lundy.*
Right: Michele Genest. *Photo courtesy Archbould Photography*

ABOUT THE AUTHORS

Dan Jason lives on Salt Spring Island, BC, where he founded the mail-order seed company Salt Spring Seeds. He has written many bestselling books about growing and preparing food sustainably, including *The Whole Organic Food Book*, *Saving Seeds as if Our Lives Depended on It* and *The Power of Pulses* (Douglas & McIntyre, 2016).

Michele Genest writes a regular cooking column for *Yukon, North of Ordinary Magazine* and is the author of two cookbooks, *The Boreal Gourmet* and *The Boreal Feast* (Lost Moose, 2010 and 2014). She lives in Whitehorse, YT.